THE ARMOR OF GOD

A Divine Defense

S. Yvonne Hall

PublishAmerica
Baltimore

ISBN: 1-4241-5922-9
PUBLISHED BY PUBLISHAMERICA, LLLP
www.publishamerica.com
Baltimore

Printed in the United States of America

DEDICATION

This book is dedicated to
My Lord and My Savior,
Jesus, the Christ,
who is My Divine Defense

Acknowledgments

I thank God, my Heavenly Father, for empowering and enabling me to not only preach these sermons, but Who also provided the time and the resources needed to organize and compile these messages into a finished work for publication.

My heartfelt gratitude and thanks to my favorite writers who have been an inspiration to me and have encouraged me to put my thoughts into writing also. Of these writers, I especially recognize my daughter, Michele R. Matthews (Author of *Raymond's Daughters*) who demonstrated great courage and tenacity in her determination to become a published author.

Thanks to my pastor, The Reverend Dr. Benjamin K. Watts, whose general remarks of encouragement to the Shiloh, New London Family, I took personally. He would often say: "there are future doctors here, there are future lawyers here, there are future millionaires here, there are future authors here with books inside of them just waiting to be written and published."

My love and my thanks to my husband and all my children for their love and support. All of you are the "wind beneath my wings."

Contents

THE ARMOR
OF GOD

A Divine Defense

PREFACE

THE ARMOR OF GOD: A DIVINE DEFENSE is a series of sermons developed from a familiar passage of scripture written by the Apostle Paul—Ephesians 6:10-18.

"Finally, my brethren, be strong in the Lord and in the power of His might. Put on the whole armor of God, that you may be able to stand against the wiles of the devil. For we do not wrestle against flesh and blood, but against principalities, against powers, against the rulers of the darkness of this age, against spiritual hosts of wickedness in the heavenly places. Therefore take up the whole armor of God, that you may be able to withstand in the evil day, and having done all, to stand. Stand therefore, having girded your waist with truth, having put on the breastplate of righteousness, and having shod your feet with the preparation of the gospel of peace; above all, taking the shield of faith with which you will be able to quench all the fiery darts of the wicked one. And take the helmet of salvation, and the sword of the Spirit, which is the word of God; praying

always with all prayer and supplication in the Spirit, being watchful to this end with all perseverance and supplication for all the saints;"

The context and content of these sermons are directed primarily toward new converts and the young Christians (babes in Christ) who may have expectations that the Christian life will be nothing but beautiful like a "bed of roses" or sweet like "a bowl of cherries." True enough, seasoned saints are often heard making these kinds of references to their lives in the songs that they sing. "Every day with Jesus is sweeter than the day before." "I've got joy, joy, joy, joy, down in my heart." "I'm saved by His power divine, saved to new life sublime; Life now is sweet and my joy is complete for I'm saved! saved! saved!" The new Christian doesn't always realize what the seasoned saints have already been through to get to the point at which they can sing these songs of victory. They don't understand that the Christian life is a daily process, and that one must grow and mature in the knowledge and grace of God. It doesn't happen overnight. It is actually a lifelong process. Sometimes new believers hear these claims of joy and peace, beauty and sweetness, and they develop the expectation that if they come to Christ, everything will be beautiful and wonderful. Before long, however, they discover that although the roses are pretty, they have prickly thorns that hurt, or they find that although the cherries are sweet, there are the "pits" to be dealt with, and very often, new Christians find themselves "in those pits" (to use the slang expression) and wondering how they got there and why.

Often they are heard making comments concerning the early days of their salvation experience such as: "I'm saved, I thought

I was supposed to have abundant life, yet I don't see any abundance coming my way."

"I've been born again and I thought my re-birth and new life would mean the death of all my problems, but problems still plague me."

"I gave my life to Jesus, and I was told that He's the Light of the World. Why does the Prince of Darkness seem to overshadow that Light in my life?"

This work will seek to address these comments and perhaps other questions that readers may have concerning some of these issues that present apparent contradiction in their new life with Christ. No, the Christian life isn't easy. It isn't trouble-free or problem-free. Here on earth, every day is not Sunday. There are (and probably will be) plenty of Miserable Mondays, Terrible Tuesdays, Weird Wednesdays, Treacherous Thursdays, Fearful Fridays and Sad Saturdays. Along with the sunshine, there will be some rain. Along with pleasure, there will be some pain. Jesus said that "in this world, we would have tribulation, but that we can be of good cheer for He has overcome the world" (*John 16:33b, paraphrased*). Living the Christian life may seem overwhelming to new believers at times, but it is my prayer that after reading this book, they will understand that because of Jesus, the Christ, they can and will overcome the obstacles and obstructions that will come their way.

In the Christian walk, Satan strives to, and thrives on victimizing whomever he can, but a divine defense empowers the Christian to resist him, to rise above his attacks and become victorious. That divine defense consists of the armor of God which Paul describes so eloquently in the aforementioned verses.

This armor has been provided for the believer so that he or she can dress for success, be overcomers in spiritual warfare, and mature in their Christian walk to the point where they can finally say, as the senior, seasoned saints say, "Everyday with Jesus is Sweeter than the day before."

CHAPTER 1

Introduction

If ever there was a need for the Christian population to heed the admonition of the apostle Paul in Ephesians 6:10-12, that time is now. Paul says in these verses that *"we wrestle not against flesh and blood, but against principalities and powers, against rulers of the darkness of this world, against spiritual wickedness in high places."*

Just exactly what does Paul mean by this? What are principalities and powers? Who are the rulers of the darkness of this world? What is spiritual wickedness in high places?

In the context in which this passage is written, in Paul's mind, the rulers of the darkness of this world were the evil spirits who filled the air and were determined to do men harm. Principalities, powers, authorities, world-rulers are all names for different classes of these evil spirits. *(Barclay-Ephes. Pg 182).* On the other hand, when examining this passage in light of much of the activity in today's society, along with being a description of the rulers of the darkness of this world, those words also describe many people who are officials in positions of power and leadership but who have no Christian standards, no moral ethics, and no personal integrity. These unethical, immoral powers which are ruling principalities lead to spiritual wickedness in high places.

Paul uses the word "wrestle" to describe the form of combat in which we are engaged. The American Heritage Dictionary defines "wrestling" as the *"act of fighting by grappling and attempting to throw one's opponent to the ground; the act of struggling to solve or master."* It is not my intention to contradict Paul, but living in this 21st century, far removed from the time of Paul's writing (about A.D. 60), I suggest that according to this definition, the term "wrestling" does not adequately describe this combat. It would seem that we are actually engaged in a full-scale war.

The American Heritage Dictionary defines war as: (1) A state or period of armed conflict between nation or state; (2) A determined struggle or attack; (3) A condition of antagonism or conflict. The verb form "to war" means to struggle, contend, or fight. Both actions—wrestling and warring—bear the connotation of conflict and struggle, but the former brings to mind a struggle in unarmed conflict, while the latter seems to imply a struggle in armed conflict. However, since Paul proceeds to describe and prescribe a full set of armor for our use in Christian combat, perhaps from his perspective, the terms "wrestling" and "warring" in this context are interchangeable. Whatever the term used to describe the conflict or the combat, Paul wants it to be understood that the Christian life is, indeed, a battleground.

Undoubtedly, the comparison of the Christian life to a battleground will be a difficult concept for the new believer to grasp, and an impossible concept for the carnal mind. After all, pastors, preachers, evangelists, missionaries—all witnesses to the gospel of Jesus, the Christ, are busily proclaiming the "good news." They constantly extol the virtues of salvation and deliverance. They teach and preach the love of God, the forgiveness of sin, the benefits of salvation, the efficacy of faith, the power of prayer, and the availability of the abundant life. Conversely, a battleground means fighting and struggling. With all of this "good news", one might ask the questions: Why must there be fighting and struggling? Why is it necessary to do battle? With all of this "good news", what, exactly, is the cause of the conflict? New believers may see what they would probably politely call "contradiction" here, contradiction between the ideal and the real; contradiction between the promised and the present. They may even be tempted to question the integrity of those who have proclaimed the "good news", charging them with false representation or misrepresentation. I am convinced that this apparent contradiction is one of the reasons why some new believers fall away from the faith. They've heard about eternal life in the hereafter. They've heard about the abundant life in the here and now. They're not too concerned about the hereafter, it's not time for that yet. But so far, they have not realized any abundance in the here and now, at least not any abundance of goodness and/ or prosperity. There has, however, been an abundance of negativity in the attitude of some of their friends. Some negativity has manifested itself in what was previously a good relationship. In other words, now that they have committed their life to Christ, instead of everything becoming better (which is what they thought they heard being promised), things are not better. In fact, things seem to be worse. So, some begin to say to themselves: "I don't need this. I was doing better before," and they drift back into the world convinced that Christians are full of contradictions (to put it politely), and that Christianity causes too much conflict.

In reality, however, there is no contradiction. Paul understood very well the dualism that is existent in the human experience, and it is the responsibility of church leaders—pastors, ministers, evangelists, missionaries—to begin teaching the new believer this concept as well. A new believer is no different from a newborn baby. As it is in the natural, so it is in the spiritual. A newborn baby has to be nourished and nurtured (fed and loved), and taught and trained in order to grow and learn and become a mature, healthy human being. If this nourishing, nurturing, teaching and training process is not done in the life of a baby, the child will die. Likewise, a new Christian must be nourished and nurtured (fed from the Word and loved by his/her new family) in order to grow and learn and become a mature Christian. If this process isn't put in place, the new believer will die spiritually.

The Biblical record says that in the beginning, God formed man from the dust of the earth. He created him in His image and after His likeness, and then He blew into him the breath of life and man became a living soul *(Genesis 2:7)*. Being created in the image and likeness of God, coming to life because of the very breath of God, identifies the divinity of God within humankind. We have been endowed by our Creator with divine characteristics, divine qualities and divine traits. Antithetically, however, God's original creation, Adam, through an act of disobedience, compromised his divine nature. Consequently, humankind fell from Grace into depravity and all future generations have been conceived in sin and brought forth in iniquity. While we are indeed endowed with divine characteristics, qualities, and traits, we also have some "devilish" characteristics, qualities, and traits that are diametrically opposed to the divine. Thus, we have a dual nature—the human nature that caters to the lusts of the flesh and produces unrighteousness, and the divine nature that blesses the spirit and produces righteousness. This dual nature—human nature against the divine nature—is a constant cause of conflict, and these conflicting entities define the "war" within us. The Apostle Paul describes it this way: He says that "in my flesh, dwells no good thing...and the good that I would do, I don't do; and the evil which I would not do, that is what I do. When I would do good, evil is present on every hand." *(Romans 7:15)*. The Apostle Paul spoke these words in his letter to the believers in the church at Rome. In this discourse, Paul had assumed the posture of a defense attorney and was in the midst of a long and intricate explanation concerning the schizophrenic nature of the relationship between the law and sin. Basically, Paul was saying that God's law is good; God's law is holy; God's law is necessary, but conversely, God's law produces sin. How does it produce sin? In two ways. First of all, the law identifies sin. Without the law, there is no sin. Sin is a transgression of the law, so—no law, no sin. Secondly, the law makes sin that much more attractive. Anything that is restricted is that much more interesting and desirable.

So then, one might ask, why have laws if laws cause us to sin? And I would submit to you that without the law, we would encounter the same situation that existed in the days when "there was no king in Israel and everyone did that which was right in his own eyes." *(Judges 17:6)* With no law, everyone would do what they felt was right in their own eyes, and that could lead to great conflict, and even more than conflict—great peril. For example, if there were no traffic laws, at an intersection with no stop lights or stop signs, who would have the right-of-way? Who should go first? Certainly everyone cannot safely move forward at the same time. Under regular driving conditions, drivers would drive without seatbelts, drive as fast or as slowly as they wanted to, or they could turn without signaling to let the driver behind them or coming toward them know they are going to turn. Imagine what it would be like if there were no laws governing the disposal of garbage. Streets and roadways would be disgustingly cluttered and waterways would be sickeningly polluted. As it is, law-keepers are too often negatively impacted and adversely affected by the law-breakers. Laws, as we know them today, are not only good, but necessary. Paul is also saying that the law of God is good and it is necessary, but it is this very law that produces sin and causes a struggle which is what Paul was referring to when he said "when I would do right (obey the law), sin (evil), with all of its seductiveness, is present on every hand."

This constant inner conflict of truth warring against untruth, righteousness warring against unrighteousness, good warring against evil, is a struggle that plagues the Christian on a daily basis. One of the reasons for this conflict is that prior to a Christian's becoming a Christian, prior to the conversion experience in Jesus, the Christ, the human nature had control. The seeds of the divine nature were present, but lay dormant; yet the seeds of human nature were present, alive, and active even from birth. A baby just naturally yields to the demands of its flesh. When babies are hungry, they cry and will not stop crying until their hunger is satisfied. When the babies feel the need to relieve themselves, they just do what comes naturally. Thus we see the beginnings of the conflict. In due time, parents must begin fulfilling their responsibility of teaching their child how to control their natural urges; teaching their child that there is a time to eat, and crying won't bring the food any faster; teaching their child that there is a certain place that one goes to relieve himself/herself, and to yield to that urge outside of that place is inappropriate and unacceptable. This is not to say that babies are sinful or evil. Quite the contrary. While babies (all humankind) are conceived in sin and born in iniquity, they are also born in innocence and ignorance (if you will)—they don't know any better. And although the human nature (the flesh) is in control, it is the parents' responsibility to teach their children how to control their human nature.

To take this even further, babies grow into toddlers, walking around and getting into everything. As parents continue teaching with the constant use of "no, don't touch", "no, don't go there", "no, you may not have that right now", etc., while the toddlers are learning the difference between right and wrong, good and bad, they also learn very early how to lie and to be sneaky and deceptive in order to keep doing what they want whether it's right or wrong. Somehow, their baser instincts and desires overrule their parents' teaching, and the flesh is determined to have its way. As the children get older, the conflict continues. On the playground we can hear: "if you hit me, I'll hit you back." "If you

21

knock me down, when I get up, I'll knock you down." And sadly enough, in the society in which we live today, in the classroom we now hear: "If you give me a bad grade on my test, I'll pull out my gun and shoot you," or "If you send me to the principal's office, I'll come back and blow up the school." Humanity—the flesh—still in control, but paradoxically, out of control and running rampant because there is no governing force to pull in the reins. And this behavior (or misbehavior) continues until the seeds of the divine nature, already resident within humankind but lying dormant, are brought to life by the power of the Holy Spirit after the conversion experience in Jesus Christ. Then, it's at the point when the Holy Spirit takes control, that the war is on. The human nature (the flesh) has been in control all of this time, now the divine nature (the Spirit) has moved into human nature's territory and literally taken over. This is what happens when one sells out to Jesus. Hallelujah! The things we used to do, we don't do anymore. The places we used to go, we don't go anymore. The things we used to say, we don't say anymore. It's not just that we don't do, or that we don't go, or that we don't say, but that we don't even **want** to do, or go, or say. We have no desire to do those things or go to those places or say those things. The Holy Spirit has redirected our focus and fixed it on the eternal. He has redirected our desires and turned them away from sin. That definitely does not bode well with the enemy, and the human nature is not going to let this go by without a fight. I repeat, THE WAR IS ON!!! and I remind you of Paul's words: "When I would do right, evil is present on every hand."

It is no wonder that Paul understood so well the spiritual warfare that the Christian faces on a regular basis. At the time that

Paul wrote about this armor in preparation for spiritual warfare, he was in a Roman jail chained by the wrist to a Roman soldier. Night and day a soldier was there to ensure that he would not escape. And as Paul took note of the soldier's armor, it brought a picture to his mind and suggested to him that the Christian has armor also, and piece by piece, Paul took the armor of the Roman soldier and translated it into Christian terms (Barclay, 1976). He equated the soldier's girdle (the belt with which he girded his loins) to Truth; the soldier's breastplate to Righteousness; the soldier's shoes to the Gospel of the Preparation of Peace; the soldier's shield to Faith; the soldier's helmet to Salvation, and the soldier's sword to the Word of God.

What marvelous imagery! Paul's observation of the Roman soldier outfits the Christian in solid armor and dresses him/her for success in spiritual warfare. God's Armor: A Divine Defense.

CHAPTER 2

The Girdle of Truth

Ephesians 6:14—"Stand therefore,
having girded your waist with truth…"

It is no accident that the first piece of armor Paul advises believers to put on is the Girdle or the belt of Truth. Truth is fundamentally a foundation upon which everything is based. In Paul's time, when he spoke of "girding the loins", he was talking about putting on what was sometimes referred to as a "loincloth" or a "waistcloth" or a "belt" or a "girdle". In the context of this passage of scripture, the soldier's tunic was a long garment, and the girdle or belt was used to girt or secure the tunic around the waist and give the soldier more freedom of movement. Girding one's loins was to prepare for action. In a more contemporary context, the girdle may be defined as a belt, sash or band worn around the waist, or a supporting undergarment worn over the waist and hips. Girdle is the image that works best for a woman with a present-day understanding of the word "girdle", and it seems to be most appropriate. The picture that readily comes to mind is that of an undergarment—a foundation garment, if you will, that is worn, primarily for support of the lower back.

Over the last few years, in many places of employment where lifting is a necessity, people who are employed in positions that require a lot of lifting, pulling, and moving, are being required to wear a large wide belt that is worn over the clothes and fits over the lower back area and is held in place by shoulder straps and a velcro closing. This piece of equipment is necessary to ensure the workers' safety and protection against injury to parts of their body. This belt is designed to support the lower extremity against the pressure of lifting, pushing and pulling.

This may very well have been the idea that Paul had in mind when he was saying "having your loins girded about with truth" for to "gird ones' loins" was to prepare oneself for a test of readiness, strength, and endurance. And to have one's loins girded with truth is to be prepared with the foundation and support needed to endure, whether it be *lifting* up the Word of God, or *pushing* against the obstacles of the devil, or *pulling* one's fellowman up out of the valley of Acor (trouble).

Not only is this piece of armor—this truth—the preparation for endurance, it is also support for another piece of the armor prescribed by Paul—THE SWORD OF THE SPIRIT. In researching this particular passage of scripture, one commentary described the girdle part of the armor as a belt upon which a soldier hung his sword (Barclay, 1976). So, for the Christian, it might be said that the girdle of truth is a **FOUNDATION** upon which the Sword of the Spirit hangs, or upon which the Word of God stands.

When we look at the word "foundation" in a more general sense—that is to say, as the base structure upon which houses and buildings are erected, we see that the base structure is intended to be strong, solid, sturdy, and substantial. And the strength and sturdiness of this structure is found in the elements that go into the mixture in preparation of the foundation. Now I'm not a mason, but it's my understanding that in preparing a concrete foundation, the process calls for a combination of the elements of cement, sand, gravel, and water. And this same combination of elements might be used when we lay a foundation of truth. We need a concrete mixture that contains some cement of reality, some sand of sincerity, some gravel of honesty, and all of that needs to be mixed together with some water of the Holy Spirit. We want to be sure that our foundation is free from any flaws. We don't want any cracks or separations or puckers. In other words, our foundation of truth must be free from lies and deceit. It must be free from embellishments and exaggerations. It must be just a pure mixture of the concrete of truth. Paul is saying that girding one's loins with truth means that one must be ready, at all times, to speak the truth, the whole truth, and nothing but the truth, if you will. Nevertheless, we must keep in mind that the admonition to speak the truth at all times is not an allowance or permission to use truth to hurt people's feelings, nor is it a license to gossip. It is, however, a premise upon which Christian character is built, and if our sword is strategically attached to the girdle in readiness for use at all times, the truth of the Word of God will be a sure foundation and a strong defense against the deceitfulness and temptations of the enemy.

Too often, we have the mistaken idea that in order to get the best of, or get back at, someone, we've got to swear and cuss or call people out of their names, or talk about their mommas and their daddies. I know it sometimes makes us feel better to do that, but in the meantime, we are setting ourselves up to get hurt, and not just getting our feelings hurt, but possibly getting physically hurt. People have been murdered for some of the things they have allowed to come out of their mouths. Not only are we setting ourselves up for physical hurt, but we're also setting ourselves up for spiritual disfavor. The kind of anger that causes us to sin in word also causes serious damage to our relationship with our Heavenly Father. And in the final analysis, we've got to go back to the person (or people) and ask for forgiveness, and then we've got to go to God and ask Him for forgiveness as well. The Word of God says: "...if you bring your gift to the altar, and there remember that your brother has something against you, leave your gift there before the altar, and go your way. First be reconciled to your brother, and then come and offer your gift." *(Matthew 5:23, 24)*. The truth is, had we been armed with the truth, and ready to use the word of God (because the writer of Hebrews declares that the Word of God is sharper than any two-edged sword), the truth of God's Word would have cut our attacker to the quick, given us the victory, and we wouldn't have to apologize either.

Now, if somebody has some doubts about the effectiveness of this piece of armor, let me remind you of Jesus when he was in the wilderness and was tempted by Satan. You remember the story, don't you? Jesus had been baptized and was led by the Spirit into the wilderness to be tested by the devil, and three times the devil tempted Him. *(Matthew 4:3)* The first time the tempter came to him, he said, "If you be the Son of God, command that these stones be made bread". And Jesus said: "It is written, 'Man shall not live by bread alone, but by every word that proceeds out of the mouth of God'" *(Matthew 4:4)*.

The second time, the devil took him up into the holy city, and set him on a pinnacle of the temple, and said to him, "If you be the Son of God, cast yourself down: for it is written, He shall give his angels charge concerning thee: and in their hands they shall bear thee up, lest at any time you dash your foot against a stone." But again Jesus said: "It is written, 'Thou shall not tempt the Lord thy God'" *(Matthew 4:6, 7)*.

Once more, the devil took him up into an exceeding high mountain, and showed him all the kingdoms of the world, and the glory of them; and said unto him, "All these things will I give thee, if thou wilt fall down and worship me." But Jesus said 'Get thee hence, Satan: for it is written, Thou shall worship the Lord thy God, and him only shall thou serve.' And the devil left Jesus, and angels came and ministered to him. *(Matthew 4:8-11)* It is imperative that we have our loins girded with truth and our swords at the ready so that in times of anger or temptation, like Jesus, we can speak out, but not sin.

Not only is truth a foundation, but truth brings **FREEDOM**. Jesus said "Ye shall know the truth and the truth will make you free." *(John 8:32)* Yet, believe it or not, some people don't know the truth. When people begin to lie, usually they have to continue telling lies to cover up the first lie, and before long, they find themselves in a quandry because they can't remember which lie they told last, and so they become confused and begin contradicting themselves. But if you know the truth and if you tell the truth—tell it just like it is right down the line, it doesn't matter how many times you have to repeat the story. You can tell it the same way every time, and you are free from that kind of confusion. You are free from contradiction.

So many people today are not free. They are bound by the lies they tell, they are in bondage to their own deceit, pretenses, and phoniness, and, unfortunately, some folk have lied so much, they wouldn't know the truth if it were staring them in the face.

Not only are there folk who don't know truth insofar as determining what's true and what's untrue, but there are many people who are still "...conforming to the ways of the world and have not become transformed by the renewing of their mind" *(Romans 12:2)*, and therefore do not know the truth that will make them free. There is a secular truth, a worldly truth, if you will, a truth that comes from logical deductions, and rational reasoning; a truth that very easily falls from the lips of psychologists, psychiatrists, philosophers, and politicians. But this truth is not built on a solid and flawless foundation because the water that's used is not the water of the Holy Spirit, but it's the water of half-truths, double-talk, innuendo, and implications.

Then there is a sacred truth—a truth that is of divine origin, based on the written word of God, manifested in the living word of God, and governed by the Holy Spirit.

The secular truth says that we should take charge of our lives—that we are the masters of our fate and the captains of our souls; however, the sacred truth is that we are not our own—that we've been bought with a price.

The secular truth says that our bodies are our own, and we can do with them as we please. We can abuse them with unhealthy substances if we want to; we can neglect them and not keep them clean if we don't feel like it. We can cloud our minds with false doctrine. We can engage in unnatural acts if we want to. But the sacred truth is that our bodies are the temple of the Holy Spirit and the Holy Spirit will not dwell in an unclean temple. We must "present our bodies a living sacrifice unto God, holy, acceptable which is our reasonable service." *(Romans 12:1)*

The world would have us believe that healing of the body is dependent solely on medical science, and modern technology; but the Word of God declares that we are healed by the stripes of the suffering savior. I'm not saying that we shouldn't go to the doctor or to the hospital or that we shouldn't take medicine. But I am saying unwaveringly and unequivocally, that medical science and modern technology cannot bring about healing without the power of God, but the power of God can bring healing without medical science or modern technology. No, God doesn't need the surgeons, the researchers and the scientists, or the technology, for he can do what no other power can do. But every now and then, He uses us to bring about His plans on the earth. He uses ordinary people as instruments of His divine power and Grace, and the surgeons, the scientists, and the researchers do need God, whether they choose to admit it or not. God uses the doctors, the nurses, and the technology as instruments to effect the healing that He has provided in Jesus Christ.

The world would have us believe that justice and fair play

means that we seek retaliation and vengeance against those who abuse and misuse us. However, the word of God tells us that vengeance belongs to the Lord *(Romans 12:19),* and Jesus said "You've heard it said that you should love your neighbors and hate your enemies, but I say unto you, love your enemies, bless them that curse you, do good to them that hate you, and pray for them who despitefully use you and persecute you." *(Matthew 5:43, 44).*

The secular truth says the more money you can tuck away in a bank account, the more interest you'll earn and the more you'll have in the long run. Conversely, however, the sacred truth is that the more you give, the more God gives to you. Under the old covenant, God said, "Bring ye all the tithes into the storehouse…and I will pour you out a blessing that you won't have room enough to receive it" *(Malachi 3:10).* Then in the new covenant, Jesus said, "Give and it shall be given unto you, good measure, pressed down, shaken together, and running over shall men heap unto your bosom." *(Luke 6:38)*

Again, just for clarification, I'm not saying that you shouldn't put your money in the bank and let it earn interest, but another sacred truth tells us to "Seek first the Kingdom of God and all his righteousness, and everything else will be added unto us." *(Matthew 6:33)* In other words, we have to do first things first, and the tithe, the first ten percent of our substance belongs to God, then we can earn all the interest we can on the remaining ninety percent. But don't forget, if you give God his ten percent, He'll give you interest on that also.

These are just some of the truths that we need to know, and if we really know them, if we have hidden them in our heart, they'll make us free—free from the bondage of ignorance, free to rightly divide and discard worldly truth; free to defend and practice our faith in the face of opposition, free to stand up for Jesus and be a witnessing soldier of the cross. Let's gird our loins with truth and be free.

Finally, not only is truth a foundation, not only will truth make us free, but **TRUTH NEVER FAILS**. Lies will fail, deceit will fail, dishonesty will fail, phoniness will fail, con games will fail, false pretenses will fail, but the truth will never fail. If there were more expression of truth between husbands and wives, there would be less failure in marriage. If there were more expression of truth between friends and neighbors, there would be less failure in relationships. If there were more expression of truth between employers and employees, there would be less failure in job performance. Although the world would have us believe that politics is supposed to be dirty and crooked, if politicians would be more truthful concerning their platforms and promises, there would be less corruption in high places. No, the plain truth will never fail us and more importantly, the truth of God's word—that sword of the spirit, will also never fail. The Bible declares that "the grass withers, the flower fades, but the Word of our God shall stand forever." *(Isaiah 40:7)* It's good to know that we can always lean and depend on the truth of God's Word.

The stability and integrity of God's truth and goodness is quite a contrast to our enemy, the devil, who knows nothing of truth and whose mode of operation is to use trickery, treachery, deception, falsification and perversion to convolute our lives and make us his victims. Jesus said that "...Satan was a murderer from the beginning and does not stand in the truth because there is no truth in him. He speaks from his own resources for he is a liar and the father of it." *(John 8:44b)*. Satan doesn't fight fairly and one of his dastardly tricks is to hit us hard below the belt which will usually cause us to double over. Then he will take advantage of our vulnerable position—bent over and in pain—to hit us. He will come back at us with either an upper cut to the jaw or a slam to the head, both of which could either knock us out or, at the very least, knock us off our feet. It's the trick of the enemy to make us think that a serious illness is unto death, when God's word says that we are healed by the stripes that Jesus suffered at the hands of his crucifiers. It's a trick of the enemy to try to put us back into captivity to one situation or another when we've already been delivered and set free by the blood that Jesus shed. It's a trick of the enemy to try to make us think that our works are not adequate to save us when, in fact, we are saved, not by works, but by the Grace of God through faith in the finished work of Jesus on Calvary. And all of his tricks and his treachery pales and ultimately fails in the light of God's truth, and when we are properly armed with the belt of truth and it is securely fastened at our waist, rather then becoming victims of Satan's attacks, we can emerge victorious in Christ Jesus.

In this unstable and ever-changing world, thank God for his stable and unchanging truths. "...The Lord is good, his mercy is everlasting, and his truth endures to all generations." *(Psalm 100:5)* This means that the truth that was spoken in the days of the patriarchs is relevant for us today and will not fail. And this is not just in regard to the promise of blessings for obedience and faithfulness, but it is also applicable to the admonitions against disobedience as well. Disobedience is sin, and sin is the transgression of God's law. **That truth will not fail.** "All have sinned and come short of the glory of God." *(Romans 3:23)* **That truth will not fail.** "For they that are after the flesh do mind the things of the flesh; and they that are in the flesh cannot please God." *(Romans 8:5)* **That truth will not fail.** "Therefore, if any man is in Christ, he is a new creature, old things are passed away, all things become new." *(2 Corinthians 5:17)* **That truth will not fail.** And to become that new creature, "...If you will confess with your mouth the Lord Jesus, and will believe in your heart that God has raised him from the dead, you will be saved." *(Romans 10:9)* **That truth will not fail.**

Thanks be to God, once we have been saved and become that new creature in Christ, we're free—free to enjoy the promises of the blessings. God said: "I will never leave you nor forsake you" *(Joshua 1:5)* and that promise is for me today and **will not fail.**

"...He was wounded for our transgressions, he was bruised for our iniquities: the chastisement of our peace was upon him; and with his stripes we are healed." *(Isaiah 53:5)* **This truth will never fail.**

"I am the LORD that healeth thee" *(Exodus 15:26)* was truth for the Israelites, is truth for me, and will be truth for my children and my children's children. "I have been young, and now am old; yet have I not seen the righteous forsaken, nor his seed begging bread." *(Psalm 37:25)* **These truths will not fail.**

"...They that wait upon the LORD shall renew their strength; they shall mount up with wings as eagles; they shall run, and not be weary; and they shall walk, and not faint." *(Isaiah 40:31)* **This truth is for us today and will not fail**; "...His anger endures but a moment; in his favor is life: weeping may endure for a night, but joy comes in the morning." *(Psalm 30:5)* **This truth will not fail.**

"Bring ye all the tithes into the storehouse, that there may be meat in my house, and prove me now herewith, says the LORD of hosts, if I will not open you the windows of heaven, and pour you out a blessing, that there shall not be room enough to receive it." *(Malachi 3:10)* **This truth will not fail.**

The Girdle of truth, truth that is a foundation, truth that gives us freedom, truth that will not fail, is a divine defense against the lies of the devil, and we can stand and continue to stand in the face of all opposition.

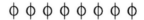

Scriptures to help the believer wear the Belt of Truth effectively

Psalm 51:6, Psalm 91:4, Psalm 100:5c; John 8:32, John 14:6, John 16:13, Ephesians 4:15, Ephesians 4:25, 2 Timothy 2:15

Guidelines for wearing the Belt of Truth

• Claim the protection of the Belt of Truth, in the name of Jesus having buckled it securely around your waist.

• Use the Belt of Truth directly against Satan and his kingdom of darkness.

• Aggressively embrace Jesus, the Christ who is the Truth, as your strength and protection against all of Satan's deceptions.

• Let the truth of God's word constantly and consistently gain deeper levels in your life.

• Then, be a doer of those truths of God's word, and not just [readers] or hearers only.

CHAPTER 3

The Breastplate of Righteousness

*Ephesians 6:14—"...having put on
the breastplate of righteousness..."*

When Paul was writing this letter to the Ephesians, he was in prison in Rome and he was chained by the wrist to a Roman soldier as assurance that he would not escape. And as he was thinking about the people to whom he was writing, he realized that for the Christian, the whole universe is a battleground, and that he or she not only has to contend with the attacks of men, but also with the attacks of spiritual forces which were fighting against God. *(Barclay, pg. 182)*

As Paul is chained to this Roman soldier who is apparently dressed in his battle armor, that armor suggests to him a picture of Christians being on a battleground dressed in battle armor as well. And so, Paul translates the literal Roman soldier's armor into spiritual terms; thus we have here in Ephesians a description of the Christian's armor: the girdle of truth, the breastplate of righteousness, the shoes of the preparation of the gospel of peace, the shield of faith, the helmet of salvation and the sword of the spirit.

There is so much rich information surrounding each of these pieces of armor that each one can be fully developed as a sermon unto itself. This sermon will focus on the Breastplate of Righteousness. I may, from time to time incorporate other pieces of the armor, but we will concentrate specifically on the breastplate and its symbolism of Christian righteousness. This message will primarily address three areas—*the Breastplate, itself, the Protection it Provides, and the Righteousness it Represents.*

What is the Breastplate? One commentary says that the Roman soldier's breastplate was the most glamorous, shiniest, and most beautiful piece of his armor. The loin belt, the shoes and the helmet were equally as important, but one didn't notice those pieces of armor first. The first thing that was noticed was his breastplate. It was made of either bronze or brass (usually brass), and it started from his neck and went all the way down to his knees. It was composed of two different pieces of metal—one went down the front; the other down the back with the two pieces being held together with brass rings on top of the shoulders. Quite often the larger pieces of metal that covered the front and the back were made up of smaller scale like pieces of metal similar to the scales of a fish. This was the heaviest piece of the Roman soldier's armor weighing about 40 pounds.

Now, the fact that in some instances, there are two pieces to the breastplate or body armor kind of negates the idea that there is no protection for the back, doesn't it? It has been said that all of the armor was designed to protect only the front of the body, and that the reason there is no protection for the back is to make a person acutely aware that he or she must not turn his or her back to the enemy—that in this spiritual warfare, Christians must not turn their back to Satan. And while this may not be a sound theological point of view, it is, nevertheless, a valid point because even when the back is protected, one still must never turn his or her back to the enemy. I want to repeat: one **must never turn his or her back to the enemy.**

By definition, an enemy is one who feels hatred toward, intends injury to, or opposes the interests of another *(American Heritage Dictionary),* and that in itself suggests that an enemy is someone who cannot be trusted, someone who must be watched constantly; someone that you always keep your eyes on and meet face to face. And one cannot watch or face the enemy if the back is turned.

In terms of the protection that the breastplate provided for the Roman soldier, according to its description—extending from the neck to the knees, it covered the chest, rib and stomach areas on the soldier thereby protecting a large portion of the front of his body as well as many vital organs located in these areas—the lungs, the heart, and the ribs along with the aorta and the vena cava—the main artery and the main vein that moves the blood to and away from the heart. The breastplate was protection for these life-sustaining organs, and for purposes of this message, I will focus primarily on the protection of the heart. You see, the heart, a chambered muscular organ, plays the major role in the maintenance of physical life as it pumps the blood received from the veins into the arteries which maintains the flow of blood through the entire circulatory system. And since we know that life is in the blood, since life is sustained by the blood that circulates and courses through the body, then it was vitally important that the heart, the organ that pumps that blood, be protected and kept in good working condition. And so when the soldier went into battle with his breastplate on, he had put on some assurance that his heart would be protected from any stabs and jabs from the enemy. The breastplate was designed to keep his heart safe and secure while in battle.

That's the physical perspective. However, the heart is more than just a chambered muscular organ that pumps the life-sustaining blood through the body. It is also defined as the vital center and source of one's being, emotions, and sensibilities. It is the repository of a person's deepest and sincerest feelings and beliefs. In other words, one might say that the heart of a person determines his or her actions. The Bible says in Proverbs 23:7, that "as a man thinks in his heart, so is he." And in Proverbs 27:19: "as in water, face reflects face, so a man's heart reveals him." So, if a person has a good heart (as we sometimes say), that person will behave in a good way; and if a person has an evil heart, he or she will act in evil ways.

In Matthew 15, Jesus explained that it's not what goes into the mouth that defiles a person, but what comes out of the mouth, …and those things that proceed from the mouth come straight from the heart, and this is what causes defilement. Just as it is important that the physical organ known as the heart be covered and protected, so it is equally important, that the emotional, intellectual and spiritual emanations of the heart be covered and protected from demonic and satanic attacks that would cause us to think, speak, and act in ways that would cause us to be defiled.

Now, how do we define righteousness? I'm only going to define righteousness according to the word of God, because if the truth be known, any other sense of righteousness is not acceptable. People have different ideas about righteousness, but we must first understand that righteousness is something we are, not something we do. Righteousness within us affects what we do, but what we do does not make us righteous. Too often we walk in righteousness that is not of God—righteousness according to our own individual standards—self-righteousness, if you will. But the Bible tells us that all of *our* righteousness is as filthy rags. *(Isaiah 64:6)* Demanding attention and credit for the good works that we perform—that's self-righteousness. Presuming to pass judgment on others based on our own standards—that's self-righteousness. Exalting ourselves is self-righteousness, and the Bible says that "he who exalts himself shall be humbled and he who humbles himself shall be exalted" *(Matthew 23:12)*.

The righteousness that Paul is talking about, however, the righteousness that is symbolic of breastplate protection is the righteousness of God that has been imputed or credited to us through His son Jesus, the Christ. This righteousness is a state or condition that makes us acceptable to God. This righteousness is the way by which we obtain integrity, virtue, purity of life, correctness of thinking, feeling and acting. This righteousness is what gives us a right standing with God and allows Him to look on us with favor. This righteousness causes us to love God deeply, to walk with God daily, to consistently follow God's will, to have an unwavering faith in God and His promises, to not only have *obtained* integrity, virtue and purity of life, but to *demonstrate* it on a daily basis, and to avoid evil.

And so what does all of this mean in terms of spiritual warfare? Just as the actual physical breastplate protects the natural heart organ from enemy attacks, so the righteousness of God protects our emotions and governs our subsequent actions from satanic attacks. In spiritual warfare Satan attacks whatever, wherever, whenever, and however he thinks he can get the advantage and cause us to fumble, fail and utterly fall. He knows us as well as God knows us and therefore he knows our strengths and our weaknesses. He knows the areas in which we can stand strong, and he knows where we are most vulnerable and liable to fall. And, ironically, his attacks, in whatever area, will invariably affect the heart. Satan and his army of imps know how to insinuate themselves into our lives so that our heart (which, as stated earlier, is the vital center of our emotions and sensibilities) comes under strong and almost deadly attack. Through trials and tribulations with our children, through sickness and sorrow, disease and death—our own or that of a loved one, through trauma or tragedy, through disillusionment or discouragement; through fear and frustration, even through anger and resentment, our heart runs the gamut of emotions. If the heart is not carefully guarded and protected, these emotional ups and downs can cause cardiac arrest in the physical, and unless it is immediately attended to, cardiac arrest is often fatal. As it is in the natural, so too, in the spiritual. There are many folk who are suffering from spiritual cardiac arrest and their spiritual life is slowly ebbing away.

In the natural sense, to insure good heart health, doctors prescribe a basic regimen of (1) a heart healthy eating pattern that includes a variety of fruits, vegetables, grains, low-fat or non-fat diary products, fish, poultry and lean meat; (2) achieving and maintaining a healthy body weight by balancing energy intake with energy needs; and (3) participating in regular physical activity for about 30 – 60 minutes on most if not all days.

Similarly in the spiritual arena, to ensure that the Christian's heart is protected against the attacks of Satan, we, too must maintain a healthy-heart eating pattern; maintain a healthy weight, and engage in regular exercise. What does this mean spiritually? It means, first of all, that we must partake of a healthy diet of God's Word. We must fill our heart to capacity with the bread, the milk, the water, the meat, and the vegetables of God's word, because what we put into our heart is what will come forth from our heart when we have to speak up and speak out. On the battlefield, Satan would have us to react and retaliate to certain situations when God prefers that we respond in His righteousness. To respond in His righteousness means that our heart is filled with His Word—not just written Word (the Bible record), but Logos Word (the Living Word which is Jesus, the Christ), and the combination of the Written Word and the Logos Word will become Rhema Word (the Word applied to our personal lives and situations), and form the breastplate that will protect our heart.

We need to possess a balanced weight in the Word. There are some folk who are underweight in the Word meaning that they have not ingested nor digested enough of the Word to enable or empower them to stand in the midst of conflict. They're still on the milk of the Word only, and as a consequence of this malnourishment, they sometimes become confused and conflicted, and this is not conducive to full knowledge of the righteousness of God. This, then, is tantamount to their breastplate being inadequate for battlefield-fighting, and Satan gets the advantage.

Then there are those who are overweight in the Word. This does not mean that they know too much Word. On the contrary, they have studied the Word exhaustively and hidden it in their heart, but rather than put on the breastplate and immerse themselves in God's righteousness based on what they've studied, they wear a cloak of pride in their knowledge and they wallow in self-righteousness. Pride and self-righteousness is evidence of an unprotected heart, and again, this is not conducive to battlefield-fighting, and Satan gets the upper hand. Self-righteousness is like a filthy rag, and pride goes before destruction and a haughty spirit before a fall *(Proverbs 16:18)*.

A balance in the Word is achieved through the aid, assistance, and anointing of the Holy Spirit. Jesus sent the Holy Spirit that He might lead us into all truth, and he will "open our eyes that we may behold the wondrous truths of God's Word" *(Psalm 119:18)*. By the aid of the Holy Spirit, those who are underweight in the Word can move from the milk to the meat of the Word and be greatly blessed. By the aid of the Holy Spirit, those who are overweight in the Word will no longer walk in pride and unrighteousness, but rather in humility and the righteousness of God. By the aid of the Holy Spirit and a healthy heart diet, we can achieve the balance that we need. When our heart becomes filled with the "Milk" of His Word, we understand with clarity that the Lord is our Shepherd, and we shall not want. Then when we move from the milk to the "Meat" of His word, we are "no longer conformed to the world, but we are transformed by the renewing of our mind" *(Romans 12:2)*. When our heart is filled with the meat of His Word, we "love our enemies, we bless those who curse us, we do good to those who hate us, and we pray for those who spitefully use us and persecute us" *(Matthew 5:44)*. When our heart is filled with the meat of His Word, "we will not repay evil with evil because we know that vengeance is the Lord's and He will repay" *(Romans 12:17; 19)*. When we feast on the "Bread" of His Word, we urgently cry out "Bread of Heaven, Bread of Heaven, feed me until I want no more." When our heart is filled with the "Vegetables" of His Word, you may not get collard greens, cauliflower, or broccoli, but I guarantee you there are some servings of "peas" that you should have every day. Fill your heart with **patience** for your fellowman; fill your heart with **perseverance** for trying situations; fill your heart with **pardon** for wrong-doers; fill your heart with the **promises, prophecies,** and **proverbs** of God, and then fill your heart with **praises** to God. These servings of "peas" will contribute greatly to the balance and spiritual strengthening of your heart.

Finally, we need to exercise. We need to participate in daily meditational and devotional exercises for about 30 – 60 minutes (or more if so desired) every day. To adequately prepare for battle, we must enter into God's presence, extol Him and exalt Him with prayers and Psalms of praise. Just as an aside, since this is a time of exercise, assuming a kneeling position in His presence, while not required (especially for those unable to do so), would, nevertheless, be good posture for those who can. But let it be understood that position and posture, whether kneeling, standing, sitting, or reclining, is only as important as it relates to the condition of one's heart during this exercise. You see, the heart is still the main concern, and standing, sitting, or reclining in His presence with a pure and sincere heart will get God's attention more effectively than kneeling in His presence for show with an unclean or insincere heart. Sometimes posture and position are informed by the depth and sincerity of one's praise. Many times heartfelt praise and prayer will access God's Shekinah glory and thus *drive* one to his/her knees in an attitude of glorious worship. And not only to one's knees, but sometimes, because of the fullness of one's heart and the intensity that sometimes becomes overwhelming, you might find yourself flat out, prostrate in the presence of the Lord. And at times like that, it's not usually petition that has brought you to that posture, but it's praise and thanksgiving. "Thank You Father for Your love, Your grace, and Your mercy; thank You, Father for favor and Your mercy. Thank You for saving me, thank You for keeping me, thank You, for forgiving me. I praise You, I exalt You, I glorify You, I lift my hands, my heart, and my voice in total praise to You."

Nevertheless, whether on our knees or on our feet, prostrate or upright, every day we must "make a joyful noise unto Him; figuratively enter into His gates with thanksgiving and into His courts with praise. We are to be thankful unto Him and bless His name" *(Psalm 100:1,4)*. We are to "bless Him at all times and let His praise continually be in our mouths" *(Psalm 34:1)*. This exercise of the acknowledgement of His goodness, His holiness,

His mercy and His grace, combined with worship and the digestion of His Word is the breastplate that arms us with His righteousness and protects our heart from the attacks and onslaught of the enemy.

Scriptures to help the believer wear the Breastplate of Righteousness effectively

Psalm 92:12; Proverbs 10:2, 3; Isaiah 32:17; Isaiah 54:17; Matthew 5:6; Romans 3:22-26; Romans 4:5, 20-25; Romans 5:17; Romans 8:10; Romans 9:30; Romans 10:10; 2 Corinthians 5:21; Galatians 3:6,7; Philippians 3:9; Titus 3:5

Guidelines for wearing the Breastplate of Righteousness

- Put on the Breastplate of Righteousness
- Dismiss any dependence you may have on what you think is your own goodness;
- Embrace the righteousness that is yours by faith in the Lord Jesus Christ;
- Ask the Holy Spirit to effect righteous actions, pure thoughts, and holy attitudes in your life.
- Use the righteous life of the Lord Jesus to defeat Satan and his kingdom.
- Expect that the Lord Jesus Christ will demonstrate His righteousness through you;
- Affirm that your battle is already fought and your victory is already won by Christ Jesus;

CHAPTER 4

The Preparation of the Gospel of Peace

*Ephesians 6:15—"having your feet shod with
the preparation of the gospel of peace..."
(Romans 5:1; Philippians 4:7)*

As we look carefully at this verse, a definition or detailed description of some of its terms is appropriate for our clear understanding.

The Roman soldier's shoes were not ordinary shoes. They were made out of bronze or brass—usually brass—and the shoes were primarily composed of two parts: (1) the greave, and (2) the shoe itself. The greave was a piece of metal that began at the top of the knee and extended down past the lower leg and rested on the upper portion of the foot. This tube like piece of metal caused the Roman soldier's shoes to look like boots that were made of brass. The shoe itself was made of two pieces of metal. On the top and the bottom, the foot was covered with pieces of brass, and the sides of the shoe were held together by multiple pieces of leather. There were spikes on the bottom ranging from one to three inches in length. If the soldier was in combat, the spikes could be closer to three inches long *(Shoes of Peace. Dean Morgan)*.

The word "shod" is simply the past tense of "shoe"; however, the Greek word for "shod" as used in this text is "hupodeo" and means "to bind something under one's feet.' As human beings, when we put on our shoes, we don't often refer to that act as having "shod" our feet, or having bound something to our feet. Yet, in reference to horses, that term is often used, probably because of the more extensive process that is required. Shoeing a horse entails more than just putting a shoe on its foot or hoof. The horseshoe is nailed or glued to the horse's hoof, and it is used to protect the animal's hooves from wear and tear. This coincides with the earlier definition of the Greek word: "to bind something under one's feet." Early horseshoes had "calkins" or protruding tabs at the ends of the shoe to provide additional traction. So, this image of a strong, protective covering for the feet in battle is what Paul likens the preparation of the gospel of peace to in spiritual warfare *(Wikipedia Encyclopedia)*.

Peace can be an offensive piece of armor or a defensive weapon. It not only protects, but when used correctly, keeps the enemy where he belongs—under your feet. When Paul uses the word "shod" in connection with this peace, he does not have in mind a loosely fitting shoe, but a shoe that's tied extremely tight and fits snugly on the foot. And so it is that we must attach peace firmly to our lives. Peace is a fragile commodity such that, if not guarded carefully, can be easily sifted and shifted, and if we only give peace a loosely fitting position in our lives, then some of the situations and circumstances of life will sift, shift and knock our peace out of place. We must firmly bind peace upon our mind and upon our emotions in the same way that the Roman soldiers made sure to bind their shoes tightly onto their feet. When peace has a firm grip in our lives, then we are ready for action.

The word "preparation" portrayed soldiers who had their shoes tied tightly and had a firm footing. With the assurance that their shoes were going to stay in place, they were ready to march out onto the battlefield and confront the enemy. Therefore the word "preparation" conveys the idea of a solid foundation in readiness for what is to come. Paul is saying that when peace is foundational in our lives, we have a firm footing and therefore, we are prepared for whatever comes our way.

Secular peace is freedom from disquieting or oppressive thoughts or emotions (*Miriam Webster*). This definition is similar to that of spiritual peace which is defined as "a sense of well-being and fulfillment that comes from God and is dependent on His presence" (*Holman Bible Dictionary*). There is similarity between the two definitions. Saying "I have freedom from disquieting or oppressive thoughts or emotions" is just like saying "I have a sense of well-being and fulfillment."; however, the believer knows that true freedom from disquieting thoughts or emotions and a true sense of well-being and fulfillment comes only from God and is dependent on His presence in our lives. When this peace, this freedom from disquieting thoughts and this sense of well being, has been firmly tied to our lives, it gives us a foundation so secure that we can move out in confident faith without being moved by what we see or what we hear. This peace puts us in a position to look directly into the face of the adversary or a challenge and stand firm. This is God's plan for our lives—that prevailing and conquering peace will dominate our life. When this peace is firmly fixed in our mind, in our heart, and in our soul, there is little that the enemy can do to us. I'm reminded of that old familiar hymn of the church: *"When peace like a river attendeth my way, when sorrow like sea billows roll; whatever my lot, thou has taught me to say, it is well, it is well with my soul."* (H.G. Spafford)

It's interesting to note that "shoes" tightly fitted on the feet is the image that Paul has for this preparation or readiness for the gospel of peace. Two feet require two shoes. The scriptures inform us that there are two kinds of peace. First of all, there is "peace with God." "Therefore since we have been justified through faith, we have *peace with God* through our Lord Jesus Christ, through whom we have gained access by faith into His grace in which we now stand." *(Romans 5:1,2)* This peace is based on our having accepted Jesus as our Lord and Savior. When we accepted Jesus, we were forgiven of our sins and thus born into the family of God. Jesus shed his blood which paid our ransom and we were redeemed. As part of His family, we have many benefits—safety, security, shelter; we are loved, we are saved, we have been declared righteous, we have abundant life here, we have eternal life hereafter, and because of these results of having been forgiven of our sins and justified by our faith, we have a sense of well-being and fulfillment. We have peace with God!

And because we have peace *with* God, we don't have to be afraid *of* God, and although we may not be big on the idea of dying, (it's something we must all do eventually), we don't have to be afraid to die or of what comes after death because we know that we shall live again.

Secondly, there is the "peace of God." "Be anxious for nothing, but in everything by prayer and supplication with thanksgiving, let your requests be made known unto God; and the *peace of God* that surpasses all understanding will guard your hearts and minds through Christ Jesus." *(Philippians 4:6,7)*

There is a difference between "Peace with God" and the "Peace of God". Peace with God is the believer's "re-birth-right" so to speak. It's ours by virtue of our personal relationship with God, through Christ Jesus. The peace of God is a gift that Jesus left with us before He went back to the Father. "Peace I leave with you, My peace I give to you, not as the world gives do I give to you. Let not your heart be troubled, neither let it be afraid." *(John 14:27)*

Interestingly, many people have peace with God, but they are not walking in the peace of God. There are times when people receive a gift, and rather then use the gift now, they put it away in a closet on a shelf for use at a later time. This is what happens with people who are not walking in the peace of God. They have received the gift of peace but they've put the gift in a closet somewhere, and rather than walk in that gift of peace, they continue to walk in **f**ear, **a**nxiety, **i**ntimidation, **n**ervousness, and **t**repidation. Notice, if you will, that the first letters of these words put together spell **F.A.I.N.T.** People who are not walking in the peace of God *faint* in the face of trouble. They are fearful of any situation which arises that seems a little bit difficult. They're fearful of people who have strong personalities and are able to bully or bulldoze their way into or out of situations. They become anxious at the least little hitch or glitch in a plan. They are easily intimidated either by a mere look or a word of contradiction. They get nervous and to even think about moving forward is a cause for trepidation. In other words, people who do not operate in the peace of God **FAINT!** They *faint* in times of conflict and/or combat. They *faint* in times of skirmishes and/or all out war. They don't necessarily fall out, but they do fall back; they take down and they retreat, not having the stamina nor the stance of a bold soldier whose feet are shod with the readiness of the good news of peace.

The peace of God is our protective piece (peace) of armor that we need in spiritual warfare; however, our feet must be shod with both the Peace *with* God and the Peace *of* God. It really wouldn't be wise for a soldier to try to run into battle with one shoe on and one shoe off. You know that even in the natural, with one shoe on and one shoe off, a person is off balance and has to walk with a limp. Depending on the style of shoe, it may not cause a big limp, but it's enough to draw attention and it lets the enemy know that your feet are not properly shod. And so it is in the spiritual. We must have both our feet properly shod with the preparation of the gospel of peace, and keep in mind that although we can have peace *with* God and not have the peace *of* God, we cannot have the peace *of* God without having peace *with* God. Put on both shoes!

Having our feet shod with the readiness of the good news of peace stands us in good stead in spiritual warfare. Sometimes it's our protection when we have to **forge forward** in battle. The upper part of the footwear that Paul saw on the Roman soldier was very important. It protected the soldier's legs from being bruised, cut up or perhaps broken in battle. Commanding officers often gave orders that required soldiers to carry out difficult missions. Sometimes these dangerous missions meant that soldiers had to walk through rough and rocky terrain and /or scale difficult barriers. Without protective guards, their lower legs would have been severely wounded and bruised.

In like manner, God sometimes sends us to and through some challenging places and situations, and in the face of those challenges, we must forge forward. In times like these, bold soldiers do not look back, they do not turn back, but they must "press on toward the mark…" It might be rocky relationships— high mountains of marital difficulties, low valleys of various emotional experiences. We might have to sail stormy seas of sickness, go through tricky terrain of trial and tribulation. These situations will be difficult, nevertheless, we must forge forward. And in order to forge forward, we must be sure that we have a **firm footing.**

As we push ahead through the rocks, the rough terrain, scale the mountains, or trudge through the valleys, we must be certain that our footsteps are sure. We must be sure that we won't lose our footing, slip and fall. With every step that we take, we must be sure that the anchors of peace, tied firmly to our feet, hold fast and grip the solid rock.

Not only must we sometimes forge forward all the time maintaining a firm footing, but there are some times and some situations in which we are not to move at all, but rather stand fast and firmly hold our position. I am reminded of Moses when he was leading the Children of Israel out of Egypt *(Exodus 14)*. Pharoah and his army overtook the people of Israel as they were camped beside the shore near Pihahiroth, across from Baal-zephron. The Israelites could see the Egyptian army as they came closer and they were afraid. Again, as had happened time and again, they turned against Moses, whining and complaining. "Have you brought us out here to die in the wilderness because there were not enough graves for us in Egypt? Why did you make us leave Egypt?" *(Exodus 14:11)* "But Moses told the people, 'Do not be afraid. Stand still and see the salvation of the Lord which He will accomplish for you today. For the Egyptians whom you see today, you shall see again no more forever.'" *(Exodus 14:13)*

Likewise, in our own lives, the enemy comes upon us and sometimes we find we don't really know which way to turn. Should we forge forward or should we turn back? Should we turn to the left or should we turn to the right. We find ourselves in varying states of confusion because we don't know what to do or how to handle the situation. And since we don't know what to do, we need to just stand fast where we are, hold a firm position until the Lord gives us direction. Even in the midst of the situation, before it is ever resolved, the shoes of the preparation of the gospel of peace, bound securely to our feet, will empower us to stand still and see the salvation of the Lord. And in those times of agitation, confusion, despair, and frustration, we need to let the shoes of peace hold us firm as we simply stand still and "look unto Jesus who is the author and finisher of our faith" *(Hebrews 12:2a)*. The shoes of peace will assuage the agitation, clear up the confusion, dispel the despair, fix the frustration and help us to hold a firm position until God gives us His directives. And while we are waiting for His directives concerning the situation, we would do well to employ the directives He has already given concerning our peace of mind. He has already said: "Be anxious for nothing, but in everything, by prayer and supplication, with thanksgiving, let your requests be made known unto [Me], and the peace of God which surpasses all understanding will guard your heart and mind through Christ Jesus." *(Philippians 4:6,7).* He has already said: "[I] will keep you in perfect peace whose mind is stayed on [Me] because you trust in [Me]." *(Isaiah 26:3 paraphrased).* He has already said: "Peace I leave with you, My peace I give to you; not as the world gives do I give to you. Let not your heart be troubled, neither let it be afraid." *(John 14:27)*

These promises of peace are part of "the promises of God that are in Him Yea and in Him A-men to the glory of God through us."*(2 Corinthians 1:20)* Therefore, if our shoes are on our feet properly, we can forge forward into the fight with firm footing, or we can stand fast, hold a firm position, and look unto Jesus, the author and finisher of our faith, whatever is needed, knowing that we have peace *with* God and the peace *of* God which gives us the victory.

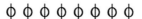

Scriptures to help the believer wear the Shoes of the Preparation of the Gospel of Peace effectively.

Psalm 4:8; Psalm 29:11; Psalm 119:165;Isaiah 9:6; Isaiah 26:3, 12; John 14:27; Romans 4:17, 18; Romans 5:1; Romans 15:13; Galatians 5:22; Ephesians 2:13,14; Philippians 4:6,7,9; Colossians 3:15

Guidelines for wearing the Shoes of…Peace
• Put on the Shoes of Peace
• Believe that you are justified and that you have peace with God;
• Wait in the Presence of the Lord until the inner peace of God which transcends all human understanding replaces any anxiety;
• Rest in the assurance that you need not carry any anxiety or suffer from inner torment or turmoil
• Daily walk in the fullness of the peace of God and peace with God.

CHAPTER 5

The Shield of Faith

Ephesians 6:16—"Above all taking the shield of faith with which you will be able to quench all the fiery darts of the wicked one"

As we read scripture and sing the songs of Zion, we find that the Christian life and Christians living the Christian life are often compared to other activities. Sometimes Christians are pilgrims traveling through a waste-howling wilderness. Sometimes life is like a highway, and Christians are like motorists traveling the interstate on their way to the promised land. Some times, life is like a sea, and Christians are like ships, sometimes sailing on calm and balmy waters and at other times tossed and driven and battered by the winds and waves of adversity. One hymn writer depicted it this way: Life is like a mountain railroad and Christians are passengers on the train that's making its run from the cradle to the grave. (Life's Railway to Heaven. Abbey/Tillman).

The Apostle Paul often makes the analogy that life is like a race course and Christians are runners in the big race. Another of Paul's comparisons is that the Christian life is a battlefield and Christians are soldiers in the army of God. This is what we find here in this 6th chapter of Ephesians. It is believed that Paul wrote this letter from prison and its message is generally applicable to all Christians, the main theme being the nature, the character, and the destiny of the Christian Church. Here, in the final chapter of this letter, he closes by reminding them that they are ever engaged in an unending conflict with Satan and the powers of evil.

It is here that we can see just how contemporary and applicable this letter is, for we as Christians, now in the 21st century are just as much (if not more so) engaged in spiritual warfare. As we look around us at the society in which we live and the situations with which we are confronted today, there is a full-scale war going on, and it's worse now because the world's value system leaves much to be desired. From the Christian's perspective, those who have been saved by the Grace of God and have become enlightened by the Word of God, and are endeavoring to be obedient to the Will of God, the world's standards are as near nothing as nothing can be. We are very much aware of the rules by which the world governs itself today.

The Word says: "The Lord is my Shepherd, I shall not want."

The world says: "I am my own shepherd, I take and I do what I want;"

The Word says: "Do unto others as you'd have them do unto you."

The world says: "do unto others before they do unto you."

The Word says: "Honor thy Father and Mother...", but in the world today, honor and respect for parents are the exception rather than the rule. Children, not teen-agers, mind you, but children who haven't even reached their teens are on the streets late hours of the night, prostituting, selling drugs, and just generally hanging out, and they will look you straight in your eye and tell you where to go if you dare to challenge them. There's a war going on.

In a society that has taken prayer out of school and put condoms in school, there's a war going on.

In a society that condones abortion—the killing of unborn babies, there's a war going on.

In a society that allows slander to the detriment of persons' reputations based on the first amendment right of free speech, there's a war going on.

In a society where stereotypical behavior attributed to certain people based on race and gender is cause for physical abuse and assault, while high-powered white collar crime is excused with a slap on the wrist, there's a war going on.

Paul talks about this very situation when he says we wrestle not against flesh and blood, but against principalities, against powers, against the rulers of the darkness of this world and against spiritual wickedness in high places. Yes, indeed, there's a war going on, on the battlefield of life, but thanks be to God, Paul tells us what we can do to hold our own as we come up against the adversary. Hence, we have the very familiar words: "Put on the whole armor of God that you may be able to withstand in the evil day..."

A very important part of that armor is the Shield of Faith. According to Paul, this is the piece that will enable us to "quench all the fiery darts of the wicked one." The Greek word that Paul uses for shield (Thureos) is a word that is used, not for a small round shield, but rather for a large, oblong shield which was characteristic of the heavily armed warrior of that time who was ready for battle. When we hear the word "shield," the word that immediately comes to my mind is protection—protection from something or someone. There used to be (and may still be) something called "dress *shields*" that ladies used to wear to protect their blouses and dresses from underarm perspiration stains. There is a well-known product on the market called "sunscreen" which serves as a *shield* or protection from the cancer-causing rays of the sun. We wear sunglasses to *shield* our eyes from the sun. We wear raincoats, boots and/or rubbers and carry umbrellas to *shield* ourselves from the rain. The places that we call home *shield* us from the outside elements such as stormy weather, excessive heat, excessive cold, etc. Alarm systems are supposed to *shield* our homes and cars against burglary. I used the phrase "supposed to shield our homes and cars" because due to the "war" that is going on nowadays, some shields (burglar alarms) are not 100% effective. There are those whose creed is "The Lord is my Shepherd and I take what I want," and if we're trusting in our burglar alarms against those persons, our shields are not always 100% effective. On the other hand, if our trust is in the Lord, then the shield that Paul is talking about is always effective if we know to use it—and how to use it.

The shield as a piece of armor was actually two pieces of wood glued together. It was held in the hand or attached to the arm and was used to ward off blows from projectiles—darts or swords. It is said that one of the most dangerous weapons of ancient warfare was the fiery dart. This was a dart that had been dipped in pitch or a tar-like substance, and then set afire and thrown at its target. As it fell closer to the target, the experienced warrior would deftly maneuver the shield to ward off the attack thereby protecting himself from critical injury and possibly death.

This is the picture that Paul presents to us as Christians on the battlefield of life. The truth be told, it is a clear and accurate picture, for out there on that battlefield with us is the enemy— big, bad, bold, brazen, and bodacious, and brother man has got darts for days—not just a handful, but a "Santa Claus toy bag" full, and he hurls them at his target at will—sometimes one by one—sometimes, seemingly, by the handfuls. Paul says, in order to counteract or ward off these attacks, we need the shield of faith.

I've already defined the shield, but how does that definition relate to faith?" How can faith be regarded as a "shield", a form of protection? First of all, as with the literal shield described (which was two pieces of wood glued together), so it is with faith as a symbol of the shield. It has two parts—substance and evidence—and together they make the whole. The writer of Hebrews says that "...faith is the substance of things hoped for, the evidence of things not seen." *(Hebrews 11:1)*. In other words, faith makes ones hopes, dreams, and sincere desires a reality in the heart while yet not visible to the eyes. It confirms in one's spirit what is not yet evident in the natural or the physical.

To make this a little clearer, I'll share a story that I heard many years ago at one of the Hampton Ministers' Conferences.

Somewhere in the south (may have been South Carolina, North Carolina, Alabama, or perhaps even Mississippi), I don't know, but it was in one of those areas and during the time when daddy worked in the field and Momma began cooking early in the morning. Such was the case in this story. Daddy and his son went out to work in the field and about noon time, the boy got hungry and asked his daddy if he could go back to the house and get something to eat. Daddy gave his permission, and the boy went on up to the house. When he got there, Momma had a pot of collard greens cooking on the stove. The boy asked his momma if he could have some of the greens. Momma said, "they're not quite done yet, son, but take this piece of bread and sop it in the pot licker, and that ought to hold you until the greens are done." So, the boy sopped the bread in the pot licker and went on back down to the field where his daddy was. When his daddy saw him, he said "boy, what's that you're eating?" The boy said: "I'm eating collard greens, daddy." Daddy said, "what you talking about, boy, I don't see any collard greens. All I see is some soggy bread." The boy said: I know daddy, but in this soggy bread is the substance of collard greens hoped, and the evidence of collard greens not seen." And he probably also said: "It's um…um…good daddy."

And so these two parts that, according to Hebrews, defines faith—substance and evidence—put together produce a powerful shield against the fiery darts of the devil. In other words, when the substance of a thing becomes evident (a strong reality) in the "eyes" of our heart and our spirit although we don't see it with our natural eyes, this produces a shield that is a powerful means of defense; a shield that is a safeguard against satanic attacks. It produces a barrier that provides protection, firm and solid protection against whatever darts may come along.

Now, if one is going to consider him or herself properly armed and dressed for battle, then one must know that the shield is not just an added accessory or an unnecessary encumbrance. From what I've learned in my research about this particular type of shield, it measures two and a half feet wide by four feet tall (*The Interpreter's Bible, 740*). We know that the breastplate covers the upper part of the body, protecting the vital organs, heart, lungs, etc. The shield is large enough to guard and protect the lower portion of the body, the stomach, the groin, the thighs, etc. Therefore, it is essential that as much of the body as possible be protected. And so, the symbolic shield of faith is equally essential. It too is not just an added accessory for Christian warfare, but rather a much needed armament. Faith is as important to the Christian walk and warfare as air is to breathing and life. We need faith, first and foremost, because "without faith it is impossible to please God *(Hebrews 11:6a)*. As Christians, as believers, our greatest desire should be to please our Heavenly Father, and "he that cometh to God must believe that He is and that He is a rewarder of them who diligently seek Him." *(Hebrews 11: 6b)* However, just believing that God is, that He exists, that He is all of the many adjectives that describe Him, is only a beginning point. Even Satan and his demons know and believe those things *(James 2:19,20)*. God will not settle for mere acknowledgement of His existence. He wants a personal, dynamic, intimate relationship with each individual that will ultimately transform their lives. Those who seek God by faith will find their faith rewarded with His intimate presence. *(LAB, 2654 note)*.

Therefore, to be able to fight the good fight, in order to be more than conquerors through Him who loves us, in order that we might effectively and efficiently execute the orders of our Commander-in-Chief, we must have on our shield of faith.

Earlier, I gave the general description of faith as being comprised of two parts: substance and evidence, which together brings reality to the heart's desires while yet being unrealized in the natural arena. Admittedly, this sounds paradoxical and complex. After all, how can one see a reality that has not yet become a reality? How can one be assured of something that has not come to pass? How can one have confidence in something that, by all standards of logic, reason and rationale, cannot possibly materialize? In other words, to move from the abstract to the absolute and use more contemporary and "real" questions: "How can I pay my bills since I've lost my job and there is no money coming in?" How can I believe that my marriage can be restored when my spouse has already left me and has told me in no uncertain terms, that it's over?" How can I believe that I will be healed when the doctor has diagnosed me with full blown AIDS and everyone knows that, as yet, no cure for AIDS has been discovered?"

These questions, while honest expressions of real concerns are nevertheless a demonstration of the kind of thinking that reveals doubt and unbelief, and they put your circumstances between you and God. On the other hand, an expression and an exercise of faith would put God between you and your circumstances, and when God is in the center, as it were, when God is put in charge and given complete control, then, we have that substance of things hoped for and we have the evidence of things that are not yet seen. And in the name of Jesus, we can stand on His promises knowing without a shadow of a doubt that His promises are sure and they will not fail. When we've lost a job and there's no money coming in, He has promised to supply all of our needs according to His riches in glory. Been diagnosed with HIV or full-blown AIDS? In spite of what the doctor may say, God's Word says that "by the stripes of His crucified son, we are healed." But of course, that kind of faith—that kind of substance and evidence does not come based on our own strength and abilities. In the finiteness of our limited understanding and comprehension, we tend to walk by sight. We tend to walk according to what we can see with our natural eye or feel with our emotions. If we can't "see our way clear" in our circumstances, sometimes we tend to not walk at all. If we can't stand on one side of the forest and see through the trees to the other side of the forest, then we won't take the trip through the forest. If we can't see the healing right now, we lay down and prepare to die. If we have a financial need but can't see the provision of finances, some people seek alternative means of providing for themselves (you've heard the expression "beg, borrow, or otherwise appropriate"). They may receive an instant ill-gotten short-lived blessing, but in so doing, they have turned their back on any legitimate, long-lasting blessing. Still others of us give up on our dreams and desires and miss out on our blessings as well. If, at the outset, we can't see the success of a project, we're sometimes afraid to attempt the process, and we either stand still full of doubt and questions, or we turn and run like a coward soldier, and God cannot and will not use or honor coward soldiers in His army. He calls us and commands us to walk on, to walk forward, not by what we see or feel, but to walk according to His word, and the only way that we can walk according to His word is to become familiar with His word—to know exactly what He has said and to be convinced that He said what He meant and that He meant what He said. He expects us to read and become knowledgeable of His word, and wherever there is not clear understanding, He expects us to ask the Holy Spirit to "open our eyes, that we may see wondrous things from His law" *(Psalm 119:18)*, and allow Him to make His word a reality in our lives. Then as we become more and more familiar with His word, He expects us to obey His word.

He expects us to **FOLLOW** after and **FUNCTION** in His word;

He expects us to give **ASSENT** to and **ACT** on His word;

He expects us to be **INFORMED, INSPIRED**, and **INFLUENCED** by His word;

He expects us to **TAKE** Him at His word **TRUSTING** that He will surely do everything He has said He will do; and...

He expects us to **HOLD** onto His word, in spite of circumstances, in spite of situations, in spite of hindrances, in spite of obstacles, and in spite of our feeble human sight and our finicky emotional feelings.

When we hold onto His word, the Holy Spirit will lead us in the paths of truth and bring all things to our remembrance.

The acronym for the words that were used in the previous paragraph to express God's expectations of those who believe is **FAITH**, and God expects us to walk by faith and not by sight. In the Christian's warfare, it is this faith—this faith which has come by hearing and the hearing that has come by the word of God *(Romans 10:17)*; this faith that produces the determination to follow, to act upon, to be influenced by, to trust in and to hold onto the divine word of Almighty God. It is this faith that makes our shield, and when we attach it firmly and learn to use it effectively, it enables and empowers us to stand against the fiery darts of the devil.

Holding onto the word brings to our remembrance that Jesus said "...whatever things you ask in prayer, believing, you will receive." *(Matthew 21:22),* and the shield of faith protects us from the fiery darts of unbelief.

Holding on to the word brings to our remembrance that Jesus said: "But seek first the kingdom of God and His righteousness, and all these things shall be added to you" *(Matthew 6:33),* and the shield of faith protects us from the fiery darts of insecurity.

Holding on to the word brings to our remembrance that Jesus said "...I have come that they may have life, and that they may have it more abundantly" *(John 10:10),* and the shield of faith protects us from the fiery darts of sub-standard living.

Holding on to the word brings to our remembrance that Jesus said: "...lo, I am with you always, even to the end of the age." *(Matthew 28:20b),* and the shield of faith protects us from the fiery darts of loneliness.

Holding on to the word brings to our remembrance that God said: "When you pass through the waters, I will be with you; And through the rivers, they shall not overflow you. When you walk through the fire, you shall not be burned, nor shall the flame scorch you" *(Isaiah 43:2),* and the shield of faith protects us from the fiery darts of fear.

"...above all, take the shield of faith with which you will be able to quench all the fiery darts of the wicked one."

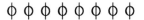

Scriptures to help the believer use the Shield of Faith effectively

Jeremiah 32:27; Habakkuk 2:4; Matthew 9:20-22, 28,29; Matthew 17:20; Mark 11:22-24; Luke 1:37; Romans 1:17; Romans 10:17; Romans 12:3; 2 Corinthians 5:7; Ephesians 2:8,9; Hebrews 10:36; Hebrews 11:1, 6; Hebrews 12:1,2; James 5:14,15a; 1 Peter 1:7-9; 1 John 5:4

Guidelines for using the Shield of Faith
• Take up the Shield of Faith by faith
• By faith, expect the Présence of God to surround you thus shielding you from the enemy's darts and arrows;
• By faith, accept God's refining purpose for your life should an arrow or dart get through the shield;
• By faith, expect ministering angels to intercept and negate Satan's strategies to attack you or your family;
• By faith, claim the victory in Jesus' name.

CHAPTER 6

Helmet of Salvation

Ephesians 6:17—"And take the helmet of salvation,..."

In the context of this text, the Greek word for "helmet" is *"perikephalaia"* which literally means "around the head" (Barclay, 1976). In physical warfare, a soldier who had lost his helmet was in grave danger of receiving severe head wounds which would (at the very least) disorient him and render him ineffective in battle. But even more seriously, the head houses that most important and marvelous organ called the brain, and if a soldier lost his helmet and sustained a very serious blow to the head, this could cause damage to the brain. The brain is that organ which regulates aspects of the body—body temperature, blood pressure, and the activity of internal organs as well as the movement of our external limbs. The brain also regulates thought, memory, judgment, personal identity and other aspects of what is commonly called the mind. And the mind is our primary concern for this discourse.

It is a well-known and accepted fact that the brain is considered so central to human well-being and survival that the death of the brain is almost tantamount to the death of the person. When we hear the medical reports that a person is "brain-dead", our immediate reaction to that news is that all hope for physical recovery is gone. And just as the brain is central to human well-being, so the mind is equally central to spiritual well-being and survival. Many people seem to subscribe to the notion that the spiritual, salvation experience is based on feelings alone, and that if one doesn't "feel" anything, one really doesn't have anything. However, I hasten to differ with that perspective. Admittedly, it does feel good to be saved; it does feel good to know Jesus as Lord and Savior; and from my own experience, when the Holy Spirit begins to move on the altar of my heart, it feels good. But the fact of the matter is that our salvation is not based on the fickle feelings of humankind, but rather on the unchanging Word of God that says, "...by grace are ye saved through faith..." *(Ephesians 2:8a),* and that "faith comes by hearing, and hearing by the Word of God." *(Romans 10:17)* This is not feeling but Biblical fact based on truth. God not only appeals to the heart but also to the mind. He says, "Come now, and let us reason together,...though your sins be as scarlet, they shall be as white as snow; though they be red like crimson, they shall be as wool." *(Isaiah 1:18)*

In the context of the text, I can't really give a full description of the helmet that was worn during a battle, but it was probably a Roman helmet since Paul was being held prisoner at Rome at the time he wrote this letter to the Ephesians, and the impetus for this particular analogy of the armor of God came from his observance of the Roman soldiers to whom he was chained. However, a general description of the helmets that are used today is that it is a head covering of hard material, such as leather, metal, or plastic. In Paul's time, the helmet was not of plastic, but of heavy metal.

As it is in the physical, so it is also in the spiritual. Paul, very insightfully, makes the connection that Christians in the army of God must put on the whole armor of God, and part of that armor is a covering for the protection of the mind, and Paul has said that the covering or the protection for the mind is **SALVATION**.

The mind is a term used for the entire complex of human's capabilities, tendencies, and dispositions to action. As human beings, through our mind, we have the capability to reason, to remember, to learn, and to form concepts or ideas. The mind is able to direct actions toward specific goals, and Paul is saying that these capabilities and abilities must be protected. The means of protection is in the salvation that has been provided by the Grace of God through faith in Jesus, the Christ.

If someone were to ask the question: "What is Salvation? No doubt there would be many appropriate responses, and those responses would have their foundation in the word that says: "For God so loved the world, that he gave his only begotten Son, that whosoever believeth in him should not perish, but have everlasting life" *(John 3:16)*. This word might be paraphrased in this way:

Salvation is the gift of God given to humankind by the Grace of God. But salvation is also an "already, but not yet" situation, and this gift is like an inheritance that has been designated in a Will. When beneficiaries are left a legacy of some kind (an inheritance), that inheritance belongs to those beneficiaries. It's earmarked for them, they have been named in the Will as inheritors, and according to all moral and legal standards, this inheritance is theirs. But until they take the necessary steps to get the inheritance i.e., present themselves at the reading of the Will, follow whatever process that has been outlined by the benefactor, and personally lay claim to that which has been left to them, they don't really have it in their possession. Those beneficiaries must **do** something to ensure that they receive what the benefactor has said was theirs. So it is with salvation. It is a realized eschatology. It is an "already but not yet" situation. Salvation is already in place. God, through His Son, Jesus, put it in place a long time ago. But until we take the necessary steps to avail ourselves of this precious gift, it's not ours yet. And in order for us to receive that gift, in order for us to have that assurance of salvation, we must believe and accept the finished work of redemption by Christ Jesus on Calvary. When we have believed and received this wonderful gift that God has given us, it is then that we have put on the helmet that protects our mind.

Now let us examine this further. What are we really believing? What are we really receiving? We are believing in the finished work of redemption that Jesus wrought on the cross. We are receiving the benefits of that work, for that finished work of redemption extended far beyond the cross. It has come down through the corridors of time to the present, and it doesn't just stop at the present, but goes on into the future. The benefit of that finished work is Salvation in three tenses: past, present, and future. If one remembers high school English classes, one is familiar with the process of conjugating the verb to be: I am (present tense); I was (past tense); I shall be (future tense). This can be applied to the process of salvation (except we begin with the past) and say it this way: I was saved; I am saved; I shall be saved.

Well what are we saying? Am I reducing the process of salvation to an English lesson? Certainly not! But for a moment, let us go back to the beginning. We know that Adam and Eve were disobedient while they were in the Garden of Eden *(Genesis 3:1-5)*, and that sin of disobedience set the standard for all of humankind to come. The Bible says that: "Wherefore, as by one man, sin entered into the world, and death by sin; and so death passed upon all men, for that all have sinned:" *(Romans 5:19)*. With this inception of sin came a penalty that had to be paid, for God had already told Adam at the outset, that they were not to eat of the tree of the knowledge of good and of evil, for in the day that they ate of that tree, they would surely die, and that death was not to be a physical death but a spiritual death. Spiritual death means separation from God, and because of the sin of Adam and Eve, our first parents, we were all born in sin and that puts us in the unfortunate position of spiritual death eligibility.

However, God, in His infinite wisdom and mercy, devised a plan, whereby humankind could be reconciled back to Him, whereby humankind could be saved from spiritual death. Back in Exodus, we see that the payment of the penalty for sin was the shed blood of a slain male lamb in his first year, without spot or blemish. *(Exodus 12:5)*

Because of Adam and Eve, humankind had been put into a dangerous position. We had been put into an awful predicament. Humankind had sinned and somebody had to pay the price for that sin. So God, according to His own law, chose to sacrifice Mary's little lamb. (*You do know that Mary had a little lamb*). He was young (33 years old, but only 3 years into his ministry); he was without spot or blemish (he was without sin); he was slain (crucified), and the blood that was shed was for the remission of our sins. In other words, Jesus, the lamb of God, hung bled and died on Calvary's rugged cross, and his shed blood made atonement and paid the penalty for our sin. This is what is so wonderfully marvelous about the God we serve. He was willing to do what He asked others to do. He asked His people to make sacrifices for the atonement of sin, and He did no less, and in actuality, He did more. He asked for animal sacrifices (among other things), but He, Himself, offered a human sacrifice. "Jesus, God's only begotten Son, paid it all, all to Him we owe; sin had left a crimson stain, but He washed it white as snow." So, it was at the cross that we were saved from the PENALTY OF SIN.

When we confess our sin, and profess our faith in that finished work, then we are saved from the **POWER OF SIN**. The Bible says: "if we confess with our mouth the Lord Jesus, and shalt believe in our heart that God hath raised him from the dead, we shall be saved. For with the heart man believeth unto righteousness; and with the mouth confession is made unto salvation." (*Romans 10:9,10*) And it's in this tense that our salvation becomes our helmet; our salvation becomes our covering and our protection from the power of sin.

Paul makes it quite clear that once we accept Jesus, the Christ as our Lord and Savior, we have entered into spiritual warfare. You see, before we were saved, there was warfare, but it wasn't personal warfare. We were not in opposition to the enemy. We probably didn't think much about him one way or the other, except when we got caught in something, then we'd say "the devil made me do it." But beyond that, we were happy (at least we thought we were happy) doing our own thing. We did some of everything we thought we were big enough to do, and that was all right with "ole slew foot", because whether we want to admit it or not, we were serving him. We were actually on his side, so he didn't really bother us.

But there came a time when all our "good times" didn't seem to satisfy us any longer. There seemed to be something missing— a void that all the partying just couldn't fill. So we began to search for something or someone to fill that void. Most of us can testify that we found what we were looking for. We found the answer when we found Jesus. When we left the enemy's camp and came over on the Lord's side, that's when the warfare sure enough began.

I know that when I accepted the Lord Jesus as my Savior, it was a wonderful experience, one that I will never forget. It was just like the Bible said: I became a new creature; old things had passed away, and all things became new *(2 Corinthians 5:17)*, and I remember thinking that from then on, everything would be all right. However, as time went on, it became evident that I was having more problems after being saved than I had before I got saved, and I have since come to realize that this is the norm. As long as we are out there with the enemy, in his camp, he has no reason to bother us, and so we think everything is O.K. But once we've gone AWOL (away without leave) from Satan's army and joined the army of the Lord, we've moved onto a great battlefield. Satan becomes our enemy and he and his army of demons are out to get us any way they can. This is why Paul admonishes the Christian to put on the *whole* armor.

Sometimes, however, when we put on our helmet, we just kind of slap it on any kind of way and then leave it unattended, and with the attacks and skirmishes and mini-battles that we encounter on a regular basis in warfare, our helmets need to be attended to and adjusted everyday.

Now, according to the text, the shield of faith is our protection against the fiery darts of the wicked, but all of those fiery darts are not aimed at the body. Sometimes darts of discouragement, disillusionment, disappointment and desperation, are aimed at the head with the intent of damaging the mind, and if we're not careful, these kinds of emotions can mess up a mind. One of the main darts that Satan uses to negatively impact our mind is the **dart of doubt**.

As we recall once again the story of Adam and Eve, we can see how Satan worked on her mind in order to seduce her to sin. He tempted her by getting her to doubt God's Word and to doubt God's goodness. He contradicted what God had said, and implied that God was strict, stingy, and selfish for not wanting Eve to share His knowledge of good and evil. Satan made Eve forget all that God had given her, and instead, caused her to focus on the one thing he didn't give her—permission to eat from a particular tree.

This is the way he tries to get to us also. He tries to get us to doubt God, to doubt the Word of God, to doubt the grace and mercy of God. He tries to get us to doubt the leading and the moving of the Holy Spirit. He tries to get us to doubt Jesus, and even tries to get us to doubt our salvation. And the irony of all of this is that He uses our own stuff against us, and if our helmet isn't on straight, we'll fall for his junk. Let me show you what I mean.

When we're sick, don't you hear him saying: "Didn't your God say that He wishes you to be in good health and prosper...? *(3 John 2)*. Then why are you sick and suffering?"

When financial difficulties come upon you and you can't seem to make ends meet, don't you hear him say: "Didn't your God say that He would supply all your needs? *(Philippians 4:19)*. Then, why aren't your ends meeting? Why aren't your needs being supplied? Why aren't you prospering?"

When it seems like you're being mistreated for no apparent reason, don't you hear him say: Didn't your God say: "He would make your enemies your footstool? *(Matthew 22:44)* Then, why does it seem like you are the footstool, and your enemies are still stepping on you rather than you stepping on and over them?"

When it seems like you're not being recognized for your abilities and capabilities, don't you hear him say: "Didn't your God say your gift would make room for you?" *(Proverbs 18:16)*. Why are you still not accepted in the arenas in which you feel you belong?"

When you're feeling all alone and lonely, don't you hear him say: "Didn't your God say He would never leave you nor forsake you? *(Joshua 1:5)*. Where is your God now?"

Sometimes when our helmets aren't setting just right, Satan's darts of doubt will find their mark and serve their purpose. So often, when the darts of doubt find an exposed place, that doubt causes us to do as Peter did—take our eyes off of Jesus and begin to focus on the circumstances, the situations and the problems around us. When our protection is not in place, we focus on our sickness; we focus on our lack of finances; we focus on our enemies; we focus on our loneliness. But when our helmet is in place and fitting properly, we can keep our focus and elevate our mind so that we can think on those things that are true, honest, just, pure, lovely, and of good report. *(Philippians 4:8)* This is why we must check our helmet on a daily basis to ensure that it sets firmly and stays in place.

Remember now, we're talking about the Helmet of Salvation. When we get saved, it's not just an isolated experience. It's the beginning of a personal relationship with the one who has saved us. It's like a love relationship. God loves us and we love Him, but we've got to work to keep the fire of that love burning. It must be cultivated and nourished if it is to flourish. And just as we cannot leave the helmet unattended, so we must not leave the relationship unattended.

How do we cultivate? How do we nourish? How do we attend to our helmet? How do we keep it well adjusted? *(I'm glad you asked.)*

Our nourishment comes from the study of God's Word. The Bible is our guidebook that helps us to know exactly what God expects of us. And as we study God's Word, we must then apply that Word to our lives; we must become doers of the word and not just hearers or readers only. *(James 1:22)* His truths are to be believed; His laws are to be obeyed; His promises are to be acted upon; His ways are to be followed, and His Words are to become a part of our spirit. We ought to be able to say, like Jeremiah, "Thy words were found, and I did eat them; and thy word was unto me the joy and rejoicing of my heart: for I am called by thy name," *(Jeremiah 15:16)*. When we get that Word down on the inside of us, we can better understand our salvation and better understand how to wear our helmet so that it protects and safeguards our mind.

I repeat, being saved is not just an isolated experience, but it's an ongoing process, and we've got to understand the process in order to properly wear the helmet.

First of all, *We are saved to Worship and Work*. We must understand first of all that... We can have no other gods before God and...*(Exodus. 20:3)* we must worship the Lord our God, and Him only shall we serve *(Exodus 20:3)*. We must be ever mindful that God is a Spirit and they that worship Him must worship Him in Spirit and in truth *(John 4:24)*.

True worship will put us on a mountaintop, or, as the hymn writer has said, it will give us a "garden experience." But whether "on the mountaintop" or "in the garden", the fact is that true worship will usher us into His presence. It will give us a marvelous experience that will help nourish our relationship. The old hymn of the church puts it this way: *"He speaks and the sound of His voice is so sweet, the birds hush their singing; And the melody that He gave to me within my heart is ringing." (In The Garden)* Yet, we've got to know that we cannot stay in the garden. We cannot stay on the mountaintop. We must go back to the valley and work, and that means that....

We're saved to serve our God by serving others. We find out from the Word that...

- We are to serve the Lord with gladness *(Psalm 100:2)*
- We must do unto others as we would have others do unto us *(Matthew 7:12)*;
- We must love our enemies, bless them that curse us, do good to them that hate us, and pray for them who despitefully use us, and persecute us *(Matthew. 5:44)*;
- We must forgive others their debts (not just 7 x 7) but as God forgives us our debts; (sometimes over and over and over and over and over and over and over again) *(Matthew 18:21)*;
- We must love one another as God has loved us *(John 13:34; 15:12)*;
- We are not to judge, lest we be judged *(Matthew 7:1)*;
- We must consider one another in order to stir up love and good works *(Hebrews 10:24;)*

But not only are we saved to worship and work, and not only are we saved to serve God by serving others, but **We're saved to Pray and Praise**.

- We are to pray without ceasing *(1 Thessalonians 5:17)*;
- We are not to pray using vain repetitions to be seen or heard by others for our much speaking, but rather we are to go into our secret closet, and pray in secret, and our Father who hears in secret will reward us openly *(Matthew 6:5-7)*;
- We are to make a joyful noise unto the Lord; we are to enter into his gates with thanksgiving, and into his courts with praise *(Psalm 100)*;
- We are to bless the Lord at all times, and let His praise continually be in our mouths *(Psalm 34: 1-3)*; and even when we don't feel like it, we are to put on the garment of praise for the spirit of heaviness *(Isaiah 61:3)*

- We must acknowledge God in all our ways and let Him direct our paths *(Proverbs 3:5,6);*
- We must believe that with God all things are possible *(Matthew 19:26)*, and that we can do all things through Christ who strengthens us *(Philippians 4:13);*
- We must believe that God will supply all of our needs according to His riches in glory *(Philippians 4:19);*
- We must believe that God can do exceedingly abundantly above all that we ask or think according to the power that works in us *(Ephesians 3:20).*

We are talking about the Helmet of Salvation and conceiving this Word in our minds and believing this Word in our hearts so that we can achieve victory status in our spiritual warfare.

- We must believe that the weapons of our warfare are not carnal, but mighty through God to the pulling down of strongholds; casting down imaginations, and every high thing that exalts itself against the knowledge of God, and bringing into captivity every thought to the obedience of Christ; *(2 Corinthians 10:4,5)*
- And we must believe that "No weapon that is formed against us shall prosper; and every tongue that shall rise against us in judgment we shall condemn." *(Isaiah 54:17)*
- We've got to know without a shadow of a doubt that we've been given authority in the earth realm to bind and loose, and "...whatever we shall bind on earth shall be bound in heaven: and whatever we shall loose on earth shall be loosed in heaven." *(Matthew 16:19)*

These are the affirmations of our salvation. And when these affirmations are firmly planted in our spirit, so much so that they greatly impact our living on a daily basis, we can look "ole slew foot" squarely in the eye and tell him like our grandparents used to say: *"You can't make me doubt Him, I know too much about Him and I'm satisfied with Jesus in my heart."* By standing up to the enemy with this kind of affirmative declaration, this is one form of resistance and the last time I checked, the Bible says: 'Submit yourselves...to God. Resist the devil, and he will flee from you." *(James 4:7).* These are the affirmations and adjustments that keep our helmets fitting properly. These are the affirmations and the adjustments that keep our mind protected and keep us saved from the power of sin.

But not only is the assurance of salvation from the penalty of sin and from the power of sin protection for our mind, but the final tense, the hope of the ultimate salvation from the very **PRESENCE OF SIN**, guards and protects our minds as well. What a glorious hope! What a glorious expectation.

In thinking about this, I thought back to when I was a child, and I remembered that right after Thanksgiving, our family began to prepare for Christmas. And what a time of excitement and expectation that was. For kids at that time, just the thought of Christmas being on its way was enough to cause us to straighten up and fly right, so to speak. I remember the little poem the old folks used to chant: *"You better watch out, you better not pout, you better not cry, I'm telling you why, Santa Claus is coming to town."* I know that I and most of the kids in my neighborhood took that seriously, and from Thanksgiving up to Christmas Eve, we were well-behaved children. I'm not trying to sell Santa Claus, I'm just trying to make a point, and my point is, that the hope and expectation of getting the things that we wanted for

Christmas kind of kept us in check and caused us to watch our P's and Q's.

And so it is with us in the spiritual arena today. The hope and expectation of what's to come (according to the Word of God) keeps our helmet on straight and firmly in place...

• The hope and expectation of the Paradise that was lost because of Adam and Eve, being regained;

• The hope and expectation of seeing the city that has 12 pearly gates and streets paved with gold; *(Revelation 21:21);*

• The hope and expectation of seeing loved ones who have gone on before. But even more importantly,

• The hope and expectation of seeing Jesus, our Savior, face to face—the one who has saved us by His Grace;

• The hope and expectation of living eternally with God, our Father;

• The hope and expectation of finally being **saved (delivered, if you will) from the very presence of sin** is the ultimate protection for our minds in this spiritual warfare.

This assurance and this hope is the helmet that protects and guards our mind, and there is really no big mystery to putting on this helmet. What we're really doing when we get up each morning is simply putting on Jesus. For you see, Jesus is our salvation, and Jesus is our hope of eternal life. Yesterday, He died for us. Today, He lives for us. Tomorrow, He's coming back for us. His death on the cross saved us from the penalty of sin. He died and He arose, and now because He lives, He saves us every day from the power of sin, and when He comes back, He will save us from the presence of sin.

The Psalmist has said: "The Lord is my light and my salvation;

whom shall I fear? the Lord is the strength of my life; of whom shall I be afraid? *(Psalm 27:1)* This is the assurance and this is the hope that enables us to say with certainty and conviction, even in the midst of warfare, even in the midst of negative circumstances, even in the midst of difficult situations, "Shall tribulation or distress or persecution or famine or nakedness or peril or sword separate me from the love of Christ? No way! No way! No way! Indeed, in all these things, I am more than a conqueror through Him Who loved me, for I am persuaded that neither death, nor life, nor angels, nor principalities, nor powers, nor things present, nor things to come, nor height, nor depth, nor any other creature, shall be able to separate me from the love of God, which is in Christ Jesus our Lord." *(Romans 8:35-39)*

Scriptures to help the believer wear the Helmet of Salvation effectively

John 3:16,17;John 3:36; Ephesians 2:8,9; **The Roman Road to Salvation***, Romans 3:23; Romans 6:23; Romans 5:8; Romans 10:9; Romans 10:10; Romans 8:1; Revelation 3:20*

Guidelines for wearing the Helmet of Salvation
- Put on the Helmet of Salvation
- Recognize that your salvation is Jesus, the Christ
- Cover your mind with Him.
- "Let the same mind be in you that is in Christ Jesus *"(Philippians 2:5)*

- Open your mind completely to the control of the Lord Jesus Christ;
- Reject every thought and suggestion from the enemy and his demons that would seek to make you doubt your salvation in Jesus Christ.
- Ask for wisdom to discern thoughts that are of the world
- Claim the victory over Satan in your thought processes.

CHAPTER 7

The Sword of the Spirit

Ephesians 6:17b—"…and the sword of the spirit which is the Word of God."
Hebrews 4:12—"The Word of God… sharper than any two-edged sword."

This piece of armor, the sword of the Spirit, was initially briefly discussed in relation to the Girdle or Belt of Truth (see chapter 2). Contexturally, the belt was used to gird or secure the soldier's tunic in preparation for action. But not only was the belt a means by which the soldier secured his tunic, it was also the place from which the soldier hung his sword.

Interestingly, the pieces of armor previously discussed are worn and function as protection for different parts of the body—

the belt to secure the tunic and give the soldier freedom of movement; the breastplate worn over the chest area to protect the internal organs in that area, specifically, the heart; the shoes worn on the feet to protect the feet and the lower legs; the shield attached to the arm to protect the body from darts and arrows; and the helmet to protect the head. But the sword is not so much a piece of armor, but rather an offensive weapon. The difference between the two is that armor is a defensive covering worn to protect the body against weapons. Weapons are offensive instruments of attack or defense in combat such as guns, missiles, or swords.

The sword (pronounced "sord") is a weapon consisting typically of a long straight or slightly curved pointed blade having one or two cutting edges and set into a hilt. *(American Heritage Dictionary)*. Paul likened the sword to the Word of God. We don't know if the sword to which he was referring at the time had one or two cutting edges. However, the sub-text for this message as found in Hebrews 4:12 says that "The Word of God is living and powerful and sharper than any two-edged sword, piercing even to the division of soul and spirit, and of joints and marrow and is a discerner of the thoughts and intents of the heart" *(NKJV)*.

The sword, whether it has one cutting edge or two, nevertheless, serves a dual purpose. Technically, it is both a defensive and an offensive weapon, for while it is primarily used to attack the enemy, it also allows one to protect himself or herself against an enemy attack. And so it is with the Word of God. It, too, is a defensive and an offensive weapon by which the Christian can both defend himself or herself against enemy attacks and also launch attacks on the enemy when necessary.

Jesus is our primary example of the effective and efficient use of this weaponry in satanic warfare as we are reminded of his responses to Satan who tempted Him in the wilderness. Satan attacked Jesus in the crucial areas of life: the lust of the flesh, the lust of the eyes, and the pride of life. But Jesus knew the Word and with each attack, he responded with the Word, saying "it is written…" The Word of God was a rebuke to Satan and ultimately drove him away.

To use the sword effectively in combat, one must first be **fully familiar** with the sword. With such a powerful weapon at one's disposal, one must have a thorough knowledge of the instrument and the power that it holds. At face value it appears to be just a handle with a sizeable one or two-edged cutting blade, yet, when handled correctly, it can produce deadly results, and one must be knowledgeable of how it works and how to work it, if you will.

And so it is with the Word of God. The full-text Bible is often referred to as "a sword" and references to Bibles that contain only the New Testament and perhaps Psalms and Proverbs are often referred to as "switchblades." Unfortunately, the switchblade isn't quite enough. It may be satisfactory in a little skirmish, but the spiritual battles in which we are engaged comprise a full-scale war and call for full-scale weaponry. To be effective in the Word, we need the whole counsel of God, and to use the Word with proficiency, we must be thoroughly familiar with all of the Word. Even more than just familiarity, one must have absolute knowledge of the Word. The Word itself tells us just how important it is to know the Word of God. In the Old Testament, Moses admonished the people, the children of Israel, to "place the words (the laws and the commandments) on your hearts. Get them deep inside you. Tie them on your hands and foreheads as a reminder. Teach them to your children. Talk about them wherever you are, sitting at home or walking in the street; talk about them from the time you get up in the morning until you fall into bed at night. Inscribe them on the doorposts and gates of your cities…" *(Deuteronomy 11:18-20—The Message)*

The Psalmist said "thy word have I hidden in my heart that I might not sin against Thee." *(Psalm 119:11; NKJV)*.

The Apostle Paul instructs everyone to "study to show yourselves approved unto God, workers who need not be ashamed, but rightly dividing the word of truth" *(2 Timothy 2:15, KJV)*.

At face value, to the uninformed, to the unbeliever, to the cynic, to the skeptic, the Bible may appear to be just words on a page (perhaps just a novel for fun reading); it may appear to be a book of mythology (fairy tales); it may appear to be just a book of related or unrelated stories with no real benefit or blessing; and for some people, it appears to be full of contradiction and error. But to the believer, it is the absolute Word of God—the word that is a lamp unto our feet and a light unto our pathway. It is the absolute Word of God which contains promises that are yea and a-men by Christ Jesus. It is the absolute Word of God that will stand forever. It is the absolute Word of God that is sharper than any two-edged sword and therefore will stand us in good stead on the battlefield of spiritual warfare.

Becoming familiar with the Word of God, reading and understanding its truths, principles and concepts is not something that can be done at one or two-sittings. It cannot be treated as one of the "books of the month" to be read within that month, discussed, and then put on a shelf and replaced by another book. Rather, to become familiar with the Word of God, one must understand that this is a daily, life-time adventure and exercise of reading, study, meditation, and memorization. And even then, true understanding will only come by the aid, assistance, and anointing of the Holy Spirit who is the teacher. It's understandable that a new believer will sometimes become discouraged when trying to read the Bible. If they begin at Genesis and attempt to read straight through, it's not long before they lay the Book down because it's not easy to make a connection between their salvation (their new birth), and the creation of the world and the birth of a nation. If they make it to Exodus, while they may make it through the Red Sea with Moses and the Children of Israel, they may still "get drowned" (like Pharaoh's army) trying to wade through the 600+ laws that were established for the new nation. Then, if by chance, they make it on to Leviticus, they will see very little relevance between the myriad of sacrificial offerings that were required then, and their lives today. We don't make sacrificial offerings of rams, oxen, goats, pigeons, doves, etc. today. Thus, if new believers aren't instructed and encouraged to read the Word in a way that will help them to *grow* in the Word and not *groan* in the Word, they will become *frustrated* with the Word rather than *familiar* with the Word, and will render themselves ineffective in spiritual warfare.

New believers should actually begin their reading of the Word in the New Testament with the gospel writers of Saints Matthew, Mark, Luke, and John (this writer is partial to the gospel writings of John for the beginner). The "gospel" is the "good news" of Jesus, the Christ—His birth, His life, His prayer life, His teachings, His parables, His miracles, and ultimately, His crucifixion, death, burial, and resurrection. The teachings of Jesus are always contemporary and relevant, and will give new believers the foundation they need to live the Christian life. After a thorough reading and study of the gospels—the life of Christ, new believers will become more hungry for the Word. In other words, they will begin to "hunger and thirst after righteousness..." *(Matthew 5:6)*. They will gradually become more interested in how it all began. They will have learned from all the Gospel writers that Jesus repeatedly refers to Old Testament writings in His teachings, and so it would behoove them to go back and begin reading the Old Testament books. They will have learned from St. John that Jesus sent the Holy Spirit as a teacher, and that when they ask Him, He will teach them and give them understanding. He will "open their eyes that they might behold wondrous things from God's law" *(Psalm 119:18)*. No, it won't happen overnight, but in due time, if one is constant and consistent in the reading and study of God's Word, the familiarity will come. And along with that familiarity will come the ability to use it effectively as an offensive weapon.

Not only must we be fully familiar with the sword, but we must **take a firm hold on the sword** when ready to do battle. When facing the enemy, we cannot afford to drop or lose our sword in battle. We must have a firm grasp on the sword so that the enemy is unable to knock it out of our hand. On the battlefield, we cannot afford to be without our sword. It could cost us our lives.

And so it is on the battlefield of spiritual warfare, we must hold tightly to our Swords of the Spirit. We must have a firm grasp on the Word of God. Now in saying this, someone might think this means holding on tightly to your Bible and carrying it with you everywhere you go. I am not negating the carrying of one's Bible. If you are a Bible-toter, that's fine. However, allow me to ask you some questions: What happens if you don't have a firm hold on your Bible? What happens if you lose your Bible? What happens if you misplace your Bible? What happens if someone takes your Bible? What happens if you forget your Bible? Remember now, we're talking about being on a spiritual battlefield doing spiritual warfare. If you don't have your sword, what are you going to do—turn around and run away? The enemy is coming at you full force now. He shot his little darts of doubt and despair at you. He shot some arrows of discouragement and disillusionment, but your shield was in place, and he couldn't do any damage there. So now he's puling out his big guns so to speak, and he's got his sword of sickness, and his daggers of disease and death, and he's got a whole tank load of trauma and tragedy. Are you going to say "please excuse me while I go find my sword. I'll be right back?" Are you going to say, "hold on just a minute while I pick up my sword?" Or even worse, will you just turn tail and run? In an actual physical battle, if you had dropped your sword just at your feet, you wouldn't even have time to bend down and pick it up. The enemy would take your head off.

And so it is in our spiritual warfare. Sometimes the enemy's attacks come so fast and so furious, there's no time to open your Bible and search the scriptures. There's no time to go to the concordance to look up a word that will take you to a particular verse. There's no time to call the pastor to give you a word. You need a "ready Word." You need a "right now Word" for a "right now situation" that will counter the attack and rebuke the enemy.

The Sword of the Spirit is more than just the physical Bible in your hand. It's more than just the written word on the pages of the book. It's a combination of the written word and the Logos word which you have studied. Now it becomes a Rhema Word in your life, and it's hidden in your heart. It's written on the doorposts of your mind. It's alive in your memory bank ready to be brought forth by the power of the Holy Spirit at the needed moment. And this is what having a firm hold on your sword is really all about— your knowledge of your weapon and your ability to grasp it firmly in preparation for battle.

Even so, there's still something else that's necessary. Not only must you be familiar with your sword and hold your sword firmly (not so much in your hand, but in your heart and in your mind), you must also be able to *wield your sword freely.* You see, knowing your sword and holding firmly to your sword will do you no good if you don't know how to use your sword. If you don't know how, or if you don't have the ability to use your sword effectively, it's like being hungry, having a plate full of good food set before you, but yet not quite knowing how to use your knife, fork, and spoon to eat the food. You will not derive any benefit or blessing from it.

To wield means to handle with skill and ease and to do it effectively. And to do this **freely** simply means to do what you have to do boldly, courageously, and without any entanglements or inhibitions. I believe in today's vernacular, the young folk would say "handle your business!"

In preparation for literal military battles, soldiers have to go through a period of rigid basic training. They do extensive calisthenics to build their muscles. They have to maneuver obstacle courses to build speed, stamina, endurance, and dexterity, and they are trained in the use of their weapons to develop their skill and build courage and confidence as they enter into combat. And when they are finally out on the battlefield face to face with the enemy and it's kill or be killed, all of the training and perfected skills come into play.

Likewise in spiritual warfare, becoming familiar with your sword (the Word of God) and holding firmly to the Word is all part of the mental calisthenics and training that is needed to face the enemy. But once directly confronted by the enemy, one must begin to use all of the training and the skills that have been perfected, and use them freely without any inhibitions. The breastplate of God's righteousness will empower you to stand. The shoes of peace—that peace of God that surpasses all understanding will help you to walk in the paths of that righteousness and keep you calm. Your shield of faith will sustain you and enable you to endure. Your helmet of salvation will keep your mind clear, and through it all, the Holy Spirit will snap your sword of the Spirit into action. He'll bring the Word of God to your remembrance and you'll be able to wield it freely.

The background scripture for this writing, Ephesians 6:10-18, is one of my favorites. I've read it and re-read it and read it over again. However, a while back, I had a problem with a part of this scripture. As the passage stands, the belt of truth begins the list of the pieces of armor (verse 14), and the sword of the spirit is near the end of the passage (verse 17). As I tried to study the parts of armor and their use as well as their relationship to spiritual warfare, my research informed me that the belt was where the soldier hung his sword. And in making the transference from the literal to the spiritual, I reasoned that the sword of the Spirit (the Word of God) should hang on the belt (should be based on the truth), and this is what caused the problem for me. If the sword was to hang on the belt i.e., if the Word of God has its foundation in truth—and I know that it does, then why did Paul speak of the belt of truth first, at the beginning of the passage, and of the Sword of the Spirit last, so near the end of the passage? I couldn't understand why the verses were so far apart, and I wanted so much to put them together—either together at the beginning or together at the end. I was so sure that the verses belonged together that for the briefest of moments, I entertained the idea that perhaps someone had erroneously misplaced these verses in translation. However, I repented of that and dismissed the idea quickly, feeling like I had been on the verge of blasphemy. Nevertheless, the thought of these two verses so far apart from each other remained with me and I knew I couldn't do anything about it because one just does not tamper with the Word of God. So, I began to talk to the Author, Himself. I asked God why those verses were situated where they were. I asked Him to please give me clear understanding. He didn't answer right away. As we are so fond of saying in our tradition: "He may not come when you want Him, but when He does come, He's on time." I continued to talk with Him about it and it was actually a few months before He finally gave me an answer. I was still working in a secular job at the time and one evening, I was to do a mini-presentation at my church. After leaving work at 5 p.m., as I began driving home, I once again began meditating on the armor and wondering about those two verses and their position in the pericope of scripture. Again, I asked God about it, and this time He answered me. He showed me a vision of soldiers on a battlefield, and as I looked at the soldiers, *their swords were drawn and ready for battle—not hanging from their belts.* And I got it!! Praise God, I got it! Then I understood clearly. I no longer had a problem with the position of those two verses of scripture. In the physical arena, swords do hang on the belt, but not during times of combat. A soldier cannot fight effectively with his sword hanging from his belt. He's already defeated. He's got to pull it clear of the belt, affect combat position, and move in.

In the spiritual arena, however, while the sword is not removed from the belt, (the Word is never disconnected from the truth), the Christian soldier must also draw his or her sword, assume combat position and move in. In other words, Christian soldiers, "draw" on their knowledge of the word with complete confidence in its truth. When the enemy attacks, they assume combat position and "draw their swords", ready to do battle in whatever situation they are confronted.

When attacked by trouble, trial, and tribulation, we can, in all confidence, draw on the Word of God which says that "in this world we will have tribulation, but we can be of good cheer because Jesus has overcome the world". *(John 16:33).*

When attacked and lying on our beds of sickness, we can confidently draw on the Word of God which says that "Jesus was wounded for our transgressions, he was bruised for our iniquities, the chastisement for our peace was upon Him, and with His stripes we are healed." *(Isaiah 55:3)*

When we are attacked in our finances, we can have a blessed assurance that when we draw on the Word of God, "He will supply all of our needs according to His riches in glory by Christ Jesus." *(Philippians 4:19).*

When Satan attacks our efforts to work in ministry for the upbuilding of God's Kingdom, we can stand firm and draw on the Word of God which says—"we can do all things through Christ who strengthens us." *(Philippians 4:13)*

Familiarity with the word, firmness in holding onto the word, and free-wielding of the word in spiritual warfare is a winning combination and a divine defense against the enemy which ensures victory.

Scriptures to help the believer use the Sword of the Spirit effectively

Psalm 119:11; Psalm 119:105; Proverbs 30:5; Isaiah 40:8; John 1:1; John 1:14; John 17:17; Colossians 3:16; Hebrews 4:12; 1Pteer 1:23; Revelation 19:13.

Guidelines for using the Sword of the Spirit
- Take hold of the Sword of the Spirit, the Word of God
- Embrace its inerrant message of truth and power;
- Ask the Holy Spirit to guide you into the true understanding of the message of the Word;
- Ask God for the discipline and dedication to memorize His Word;
- Saturate your mind, your heart, and your spirit with His Word
- Then, be a doer of the Word, and not just a reader, memorizer, or a hearer of the Word.

CHAPTER 8

Prayer

Ephesians 6:18—"praying always with all prayer and supplication in the Spirit, being watchful to this end with all perseverance and supplication for all the saints."

"The weapons of our warfare are not carnal but mighty in God to the pulling down of strongholds..." (2 Corinthians 10:4)

Including prayer, which can be identified as offensive armor and a defensive weapon, there are seven parts to the whole armor of God—(1) The Belt (Girdle of Truth), (2) the Breastplate of Righteousness; (3) the Shoes of the Gospel of the Preparation of Peace, (4) the Shield of Faith, (5) the Helmet of Salvation, (6) the Sword of the Spirit, and (7) Prayer.

According to Biblical numerology, the number "7" is God's perfect number; the number for completeness or wholeness. And so with prayer included, we can consider the armor complete and effective, and if worn properly, we are dressed for success.

Looking at this through natural eyes, prayer as armor or a weapon might seem to be out of place here. It isn't paired with a literal piece of armor as the other pieces of armor are—the *belt* of truth, the *breastplate* of righteousness, the *shoes* of peace, the *shield* of faith, the *helmet* of salvation, and the *Sword of the Spirit* which is God's Word. We could, however, pair it with another instrument and say "the *umbrella* of prayer." Why an umbrella? Because an umbrella is a coverall. In the natural when there is a heavy rainfall, we can wear a rain hat to protect our head, a raincoat to protect our clothing, boots, rubbers, or galoshes to protect our feet and our shoes. But for added overall protection, we use an umbrella which covers all and provides protection even for our face from the rain. The rain hat, raincoat and boots are effective, but the umbrella enhances their effectiveness and gives us greater overall protection from the rain. Likewise with the armor. Each piece of the armor is effective in it's particular function, but prayer enhances its effectiveness and makes the armor more effective overall. So, to put on the "whole armor of God" is to include the dually-functioning effective and protective weapon of prayer.

Prayer is such an important part of the armor because it's our means of communicating with God, letting him know what's going on with us; letting Him know exactly what we need and what we want. Of course, there is no doubt that He already knows, but His word tells us to "ask and we shall receive." James says, "we have not because we ask not;"*(James 4:2b)* Peter tells us to "cast all of our cares on Him, because He cares for us." *(1 Peter 5:7).* Paul says, "in everything by prayer and supplication with thanksgiving, let your requests be made known unto God." *(Philippians 4:6).* In other words, He gives the commands, but these commands are also permission to bring all of our petitions and supplications to Him. So then, in spiritual warfare, in times when we must enter into serious battle with the enemy, yes, we're armed, and each piece is in place, but now we must pray and invoke God's presence to be with us to ensure that we use effectively that which He has provided for us. "Father, please help me to fight with integrity. Help me to fight truthfully; help me to fight righteously; help me to fight peacefully; help me to fight faithfully, help me to fight with clarity of mind; help me to stand firmly on Your word as I fight for the right." Do the terms "fight with integrity", "fight truthfully", fight righteously", "fight peacefully" seem like oxymorons? Do they seem contradictory and paradoxical? Of course they do to the carnal mind. In a natural physical street fight with an enemy, fighters have usually reached this point because of their lack or total absence of integrity, righteousness, truth and peace. But in the spiritual arena, we do not fight the same way the world does, We are not conformed to the world, but we have been transformed by the renewing of our mind. And so in spiritual warfare, we pray that God will empower us to use our armor and weaponry according to His will and His way.

Not only do we pray because it's our means of communicating with God, **but we pray also because God has commanded us to pray.** Prayer is not a choice but a charge. It's not a request but a requirement. It's not an option, but it is an opportunity to develop a personal, intimate relationship with the Father. Listen to the Word of the Lord: "Pray for those who spitefully use you and persecute you." *(Matthew 5:44)*. "Watch and pray that you enter not into temptation…" *(Matthew 26:41)*; "…Men ought always to pray and not faint." *(Luke 18:1);* "Watch ye therefore and pray always, that you may be accounted worthy to escape all these things that shall come to pass…" *(Luke 21:36)'* "Pray without ceasing" *(1 Thessalonians 5:17)*; "I will therefore that men pray every where, lifting up holy hands without wrath and doubting." *(1 Timothy 2:8);* "Confess your faults one to another, and pray one for another that you may be healed. The effectual fervent prayer of the righteous avails much." *(James 5:16)*. And of course, in the text of this writing following immediately after the description of all the armor… "praying always with all prayer and supplication in the Spirit being watchful to this end with all perseverance and supplication for all the saints." *(Ephesians 6:18)*. Prayer is an essential part of the armor and our obedience to the command is essential to our success in spiritual warfare. When we put on the whole armor, prayer empowers us to walk in truth, to walk in righteousness, to walk in peace, and to walk by faith, not by sight. Prayer gives us the continued assurance of our salvation, and when we pray God's Word back to Him, we have the confidence that He hears us, and we know that we have the petitions that we asked.

Not only are we protected in prayer, but there is power in prayer. Talking to God, the Father, in the name of Jesus, the son, by the power of the Holy Spirit has the power to change things. It will change people. It will change circumstances, and it will change situations, according to God's will. This is not just cliché, this is not just another platitude—something that people say to encourage others. This is a divine principle and a scriptural fact whose basis is found in Genesis 18, when Abraham not only talked with God, but technically negotiated, albeit somewhat timidly, but nevertheless pressed his point with God on behalf of any righteous persons who might have been caught in the intended destruction of Sodom. From this exchange, it would seem that Abraham's conversation with God changed things at that time. Likewise, when we pray, when we talk honestly and sincerely with God, there's power and the potential for change in a particular situation. And not only can situations and circumstances change, but through prayer, people can change; hearts, minds, and attitudes can all change according to God's will. Things may not always change immediately, as a matter of fact, some things may seem like they will never change. And it's in those times of delay that our faith is put to the test, and we begin to encounter demonic attacks. We're hit with darts of doubt, arrows of apprehension, missiles of misgivings and machetes of misunderstandings, slingshots of schisms and spears of skepticism and the warfare is on. Satan will do everything he can to have us believe that since we haven't received an answer, that no answer is forthcoming, and we must stand firmly and boldly and remind him that delays are not necessarily denials. And so we combine our prayer with parts of the armor. Prayer combined with the sword of the spirit and the belt of truth gives us the power to remind the enemy of the truth of God's Word. It gives us the power to remind the enemy that "God's thoughts are not our thoughts and that our ways are not His ways." (*Isaiah 55:8*) We can remind the enemy that "we will rest in the Lord and wait patiently for Him." *(Psalm 37:7);* that "they that wait upon the Lord shall renew their strength, they shall mount up with wings as eagles; they shall run and not get weary, they shall walk and not faint." *(Isaiah 40:31).* And when we also combine that prayer with the shield of faith, we can stand against the darts, the arrows and the slings and put the doubts, apprehension, and uncertainty to rest. We can say (like the senior saints used to say) He may not come when we want Him, but He's always on time. We can combine prayer with the breastplate of righteousness and remind Satan that "[we are] blessed when we hunger and thirst after righteousness for we shall be filled." *(Matthew 5:6).* We can combine prayer with the shoes of peace and remind Satan that because of our peace with God, "the peace of God that surpasses all understanding will guard our hearts and our minds through Christ Jesus" *(Philippians 4:7).*

There is indeed power in prayer—miracle-working power, power to save, power to heal, power to deliver and power to set free. However, in order to access this power and in order to access the protection that prayer gives us, we must be diligent in our prayer life. We must, as Paul says, pray without ceasing. We must **P.U.S.H—PRAY UNTIL SOMETHING HAPPENS!.** The word PUSH, as it relates to this subject, brings to mind the childbirth experience. During the birth experience, there is a point at which the contractions become so intense, the expectant mother feels the urge—a great need to PUSH. And if her physician feels that the baby is in position and ready to be ushered into the world, he or she will tell the expectant mother to bear down and PUSH as hard as she can. She has been given permission to push, but she also now has the responsibility to push and continue to push (under the guidance of her physician) until the baby is brought forth.

And so it is with us as it relates to prayer and PUSHing in spiritual warfare. Many times on this battlefield, we are hit with problems and difficulties that sometimes feel like the contractions of childbirth (gentlemen may not understand this, but in your mind, try to conjure up the worst pain you've ever had). The difficulty may be unemployment, discrimination, marital discord, disobedient and prodigal children, sickness, disease, tragedy and death. However, whatever the problem, whatever dart, arrow, or missile that Satan has aimed at us, we can't freeze up in fear—fear won't stop the contractions. We can't tighten up with worry—worry won't stop the contractions. What will stop the contractions? We've got to begin to PUSH. Tighten our belts and PUSH. Adjust our breastplates and PUSH. Shine our shoes and PUSH. Get our shield in position and PUSH. Straighten up our helmet and PUSH. Draw our sword and PUSH. Use our armor and Pray Until Something Happens. Tell God (like Jacob did) "I won't let You go until You bless me." (*Genesis 32:26*)

When you pray and pray effectively, something will happen. You will receive the fruit of your labor. That trial, that tribulation, that problem, that burden—all of that was labor. It was hard work, but thanks be to God who gives us the victory, labor ends in the bringing forth of new life—new employment, healing from sickness (new life), deliverance from bondage (new life), resurrection of some dead situation (new life), restoration of a relationship (new life), and renewal of a right spirit (new life). Rest assured that if you pray and pray according to the Word of God, King Jesus will roll all burdens away.

φ φ φ φ φ φ φ

Scriptures to help the believer Pray effectively
Matthew 5:44; Mathew 6:5,9; Romans 8:26; 1 Thessalonians 5:17; Philippians 4:6,7; James 5:13-16

Guidelines for Praying
* Matthew 6: 5-15 (This one passage sums it up completely)

CHAPTER 9

Conclusion

Paul says "...put on the **whole** armor of God..." This speaks to the necessity of being fully and completely armed in preparation for battle. This says that **all** (not some), but all of the pieces of God's armor are necessary if one is going to fight successfully—not being halfway dressed having some pieces missing, but having on the full armor.

Secularly, the belt, the breastplate, the shoes, the shield, the helmet and the sword all have their individual specific designations, locations, and functions. However, four pieces of armor (the belt, the breastplate, the shoes, and the helmet), are to be worn as defensive protection of our body against the attacks of the enemy; one piece is attached to the arm (the shield) and is to be used strategically to protect from the onslaught of arrows, darts, and missiles that may be fired by the enemy, and one piece (the sword), while considered to be a part of the armor, is actually an offensive weapon to be used aggressively against the enemy. Technically, we are protected by the armor, but we fight with the weapon.

Spiritually, each part of God's armor has its individual designation, location and function as well. All of the pieces are necessary, but as it is with the secular armor, so it is with the spiritual armor. We are protected by the armor of truth, righteousness, the gospel of peace, faith, and our salvation, but we fight with the weapons of the Word and Prayer.

Putting on the whole armor and dressing for success is not just a one-time hit and run exercise. For the believer, spiritual warfare is ongoing, and we must always be armed and ready for battle. Satan does not fight fair and he has no scruples, therefore, we must always be on our guard. An old hymn of the church: "My Soul be on Thy Guard" *(Heath/Lowell)* says it this way:

> *"My soul be on thy guard, ten thousand foes arise;*
> *The hosts of sin are pressing hard to draw thee from the skies.*
> *O watch and fight and pray the battle's ne'er give o'er;*
> *Renew it boldly every day, and help divine implore.*
> *Ne'er think the victory won, nor lay thine armor down,*
> *The work of faith will not be done, till thou obtain thy crown.*
> *Fight on, my soul, till death shall bring thee to thy God;*
> *He'll take thee, at thy parting breath to His divine abode."*

This armor isn't to be put on and taken off at will, nor is it to be worn only when it's convenient or suits our own personal purposes. Just as our God never slumbers nor sleeps, neither does the enemy. When we're sleeping, he's awake. When we're down for the night, he's up to no good The enemy doesn't attack at our convenience, but whenever he sees the opportunity. And what opportunities does he look for? First of all, the absence of all or any part of the armor is a primary opportunity for the enemy to launch an attack. Any missing piece means there's an open door for him to come in, raise havoc and confusion, to distract us and cause us to lose the battle.

If truth is missing, then righteousness is ineffective, and vice versa; if righteousness is missing, than truth is ineffective. Truth without righteousness tends to become personal opinion, imagination, assumption, and/or conjecture. This truth has no integrity in the Word of God and can't be trusted.

If peace is absent, the evil twin imps named "Chaos" and "Confusion" take up residence in its place. Confusion causes issues to become blurry and distorted, and Chaos brings on the darkness, thereby causing visual difficulty and rendering the spiritual soldier incompetent.

If faith is missing, we're not pleasing God ("...without faith it is impossible to please God for he who comes to God must believe that He is and that He is a rewarder of those who diligently seek Him"—*Hebrews 11:6*), and to suffer God's displeasure is really not where we want to be.

If salvation is missing, we're totally exposed and vulnerable to any and all kinds of attacks. The absence of salvation means that the soul is unsaved and headed for destruction. It means that the mind is unprotected and therefore receptive to all the ideas, thoughts, and suggestions from the enemy.

If the sword is missing, the Word of God, (technically, our only offensive weapon), we have no basis or foundation on which to stand. We may be protected in other areas, but we have nothing with which to fight. "God's Word is a lamp unto our feet and a light unto our path." Without His word, we are walking in utter darkness.

If prayer is missing, we have no connection with Headquarters. There is no open line of communication between us and our Captain. How then can we know what to do—what steps to take, or what moves to make unless we are able to receive our orders from our Chief Executive Officer (CEO)? Prayer is the connection that gives us that access.

Not only does the enemy look for absence of the total armor or missing pieces of armor, but he's also on the look-out for armor that isn't securely in place. A loose belt, a crooked breastplate, worn out shoes, lopsided shield, disheveled helmet, or a dull sword. Unsecured armor is equivalent to having on no armor at all, and if you're not ready to fight, if one is not prepared to fight and fight effectively, then one needs to retreat, fall back and regroup.

The enemy finds another opportunity when people are trying to wear other kinds of armor in conjunction with God's Divine Armor. This means that some people try to "straddle the fence" if you will. They want to walk on both sides of the street at the same time. They put on the girdle of truth before they take off the dirty undergarments of lies and deception. They want to wear the breastplate of righteousness while still wearing the backpack of unrighteousness. They wear a shoe of peace on one foot, but on the other foot is a shoe of chaos and confusion. They're wearing a shield of faith on one arm as well as a shield of fear on the other. And their weapons seem to be reversed: They're carrying a pocketknife of the Word of God on Sunday morning, but from Monday to Saturday, they're carrying a sword of opinions, assumptions, imagination and conjecture. In other words, they don't have much of the Word of God, but they're real big on their own opinions and assumptions. This is a big loophole through which the enemy can easily climb and then take control. You see, you can't double dip and expect to be victorious. You can't be hot and cold at the same time. You know that when you mix hot and cold water, you get "lukewarm water", and for some people, "lukewarm water" is sickening to the taste. Jesus told the people at the church in Laodicea that because they were lukewarm (neither hot nor cold), that He would spew them out of His mouth. *(Revelation 3:16)*. You've either got to be one thing or the other. Jesus said: "No servant can serve two masters; for either he will hate the one and love the other, or else he will be loyal to the one and despise the other. You cannot serve God and mammon." *(Luke 16:13)* Joshua told the Children of Israel to "...choose you this day whom you will serve..." *(Joshua 24:15)*, and it is just as applicable to us today. We must make a choice, and it would be in our best interest to choose the best and get rid of the mess. Choose God's Divine Armor.

Finally, we may have on all the armor, and only God's armor, and we may have it on securely, but the enemy finds yet another opportunity to destroy us in our inability to use the armor and use it effectively. It's like this age of technology in which we now live, where so many folk have VCRs, DVD players, hi-tech, hi-def TVs, Palm Pilots, Cell Phones, iPods, GPSs and other technological gadgets, yet they really don't know how to use them to their best advantage. Once they find the on/off button, they master that, and that's about the extent of their ability to use the device. Anything else needed, they call Cousin Joe or Aunt Sally (the geeks in the family) to come over and help them out. Unfortunately, some of us are the same way with our armor— we've got it on but we don't know how to use it properly, and so the enemy takes advantage of our ignorance, and Cousin Joe or Aunt Sally can't help us out in this situation. They can't hook us up. They can't program and put our armor in working order for us. They can't fight our battles for us. This is something each and everyone of us must do for ourselves.

By now, I suppose someone is asking the questions, just how do we put on these different pieces of armor? How do we put them on securely? How do we learn to master them and use them effectively once we have them on? Well, the conclusion to the whole matter is just this: As we spiritually put on the whole armor of God, (as I said in Chapter 6), the reality is that we are simply putting on **JESUS!!** The armor is actually Jesus, himself and in putting on the armor, one is actually clothing himself or herself with the protection of the Lord Jesus Christ. The power of Christ Jesus is sufficient to stand against all of the evil and the temptations that the believer will encounter.

To Gird our Loins with truth is to put on Jesus. The Bible says: "…the word was made flesh and dwelt among us and we beheld His glory, the glory as of the only begotten of the Father full of grace and truth." *(John 1:14)* "…the law was given by Moses, but grace and truth came by Jesus Christ." *(John 1:17)*. "You shall know the truth and the truth shall make you free." *(John 8:32)*.

Jesus said "I am the way, the truth and the life…" *(John 14:6)*. When we put on Jesus, we have the assurance of truth—the power to tell the truth, the whole truth and nothing but the truth. We have the power to stand firm on the truth, and the ability to discern truth—to determine the difference between lies, deceit, false claims and the unadulterated truth.

To put on the Breastplate of Righteousness is to put on Jesus. Jesus is our righteousness. "For He made Him who knew no sin to be sin for us that we might become the righteousness of God in Him." *(2 Corinthians 5:21)*. When Jesus was crucified, hanging there on that "old rugged cross", dying for sinful humanity, he took the sins of humankind upon himself in exchange for his own righteousness. He dirtied himself in order that we might be made clean. He lowered himself to our level that we might be raised to his level. When we put on Jesus, we put on righteousness personified, and it becomes incumbent upon us to walk in that righteousness daily—to walk with our breastplate (Jesus) securely in place.

To have our Feet Shod with the Preparation of the Gospel of Peace is to put on Jesus. Jesus is our peace. He said in *John 14:27*: "Peace I leave with you, my peace I give to you; not as the world gives do I give to you…" Paul said of Jesus in *Ephesians 2:13, 14*: "But now in Christ Jesus you who once were far off have been brought near by the blood of Christ, for He, Himself, is our peace, who has made both one, and has broken down the middle wall of separation…" Jesus is that peace *of* God that surpasses all understanding *(Philippians 4:7)*. He is that peace *of* God that rules in our hearts *(Colossians 3:15)*. He is also the peace that we have *with* God because we have been justified by faith *(Romans 5:1)*. He is that perfect peace that God has promised when we keep our mind stayed on Him. *(Isaiah 26:3)*

To have the Shield of Faith is to have Jesus. "Looking unto Jesus, the author and finisher of our faith, who for the joy that was set before him, endured the cross, despising the shame, and is set down at the right hand of the throne of God." *(Hebrews 12:2)* Jesus is the object of our faith. He is the only reason for our faith. Our faith in the finished work of Jesus on Calvary—his crucifixion, death, burial, and resurrection—is our protection against doubt and defeat, and it is our hope for eternal life. To have Jesus as our shield is to have that blessed assurance that in whatever situations or circumstances, we shall be able to stand, and that "we are more than conquerors through Him who loved us." With the Shield of Faith (Jesus), we are [fully] persuaded that neither death nor life, nor angels nor principalities, nor powers, nor things present nor things to come, nor height nor depth, nor any other created thing, shall be able to separate us from the love of God which is in Christ Jesus our Lord." *(Romans 8:37-39)*. By faith, we will not be defeated in spiritual warfare.

To put on the Helmet of Salvation is to put on Jesus. Jesus is our salvation, "…there is no salvation in any other, for there is no other name under heaven given among men by which we must be saved." *(Acts 4:12)* To have on Jesus as our helmet is to have our head and our mind covered and protected by the knowledge that Jesus saves from the guttermost to the uttermost, and that we are indeed saved by His power divine. Now although we are saved *from* some things (the penalty and the power of sin), and we are saved *to* some things (a new life in Christ and all that that entails), there are still some things from which we are not saved. We are not saved from troubles and trials. We are not saved from Satan's temptations and tests. But in the midst of all of this, Jesus will see us through our troubles and temptations. Jesus will help us stand the tests and trials. We may not escape Satan's demoniac attacks, but Jesus, our healer, will help us to recover. Jesus our deliverer, will deliver us from captivity. Jesus our Savior and our salvation will set us free.

To have the Sword of the Spirit (God's Word) is to have Jesus. The Bible is the written word which reveals the Logos—the Living Word which is Jesus, and that Living Word is visible all throughout the Written Word by means of the scarlet thread that runs from Genesis to Revelation. "In the beginning was the Word and the Word was with God and the Word was God." *(John 1:1)*. Jesus said "If you abide in me, and my words abide in you, you shall ask what you desire and it will be done for you." *(John 15:7)*

To use the weapon of prayer, we use the name of Jesus, because it is only as we pray to the Father, in the name of the Son (Jesus) by the power of the Holy Spirit that we will receive that for which we pray. Jesus says: "whatever you ask in my name, that will I do that the Father may be glorified in the Son." "If you ask anything in my name, I will do it." *(John 14:13, 14)*. He said further, "And in that day you will ask me nothing. Most assuredly, I say to you, whatever you ask the Father in my name, He will give you. Until now, you have asked nothing in my name. Ask and you shall receive, that your joy may be full" *(John 16:23, 24)*.

Since Paul says "Put on the whole armor…" some might suggest that a good exercise might be to put on this armor each day. When we awake and arise each morning, as we prepare for the day, put on the armor. However, once we have come to a full realization of what this armor is all about and have learned to appropriate it effectively, I suggest, that once you put it on, keep it on. You might want to check it each morning to be sure that each piece is securely in place and fitting properly. Remember that the enemy looks for ill-fitting and unsecured armor as opportunities to attack. But for the love of God, do not remove your armor at night as you would remove your clothes in preparation for bed. I submit to you that your time of sleep is another opportunity for the enemy to attack—in your thoughts before sleep, in your dreams during sleep. Did you ever awaken in the morning with some kind of alien ideas or notions and wondered where they came from? An idle and unprotected mind is the devil's workshop. And so, for best results, the full armor, God's Armor (Jesus):The Divine Defense must be your pajamas as "you lay yourself down to sleep at night and pray the Lord your soul to keep". God's Armor (Jesus): The Divine Defense must be your day dress as you go forth throughout the day. God's Armor (Jesus): The Divine Defense must be worn to Sunday School and Church on Sunday morning, to Bible Study on Wednesday night (or whatever night), to choir rehearsal, to ministry meetings, to conferences, conventions, retreats, workshops, and even on vacation. *"We do not wrestle against flesh and blood, but against principalities, against powers, against the rulers of the darkness of this age, against spiritual hosts of wickedness in high places; therefore, take up the whole armor of God (God's Armor) that you may have a Divine Defense and be able to withstand in the evil day and having done all, to stand." (Ephesians 6:13, 14 paraphrased).*

APPENDIX A

A New Believer's Guide to Daily Personal Consecration and Commitment

This guide is an attempt to assist the new believer in moving beyond a head knowledge of God to a heart knowledge; to move from religious ritual to personal relationship. The best way to develop a relationship with someone is through communication, and that must be two-way communication. Likewise in seeking a personal relationship with God, there must be communication, and that communication is done through prayer and Bible-reading/study. In other words, we speak to God in prayer; God speaks to us through His word, and we must read His word in order to hear and understand what He is saying to us.

The following suggestions are simply a guide into this process of communicating with God. In time, through your personal study and prayer, no doubt you will come upon other methods and other scriptures that you may wish to either incorporate into this one or let stand alone. The key is to communicate with God, consecrate yourself to God, and commit your life to God on a daily basis which will cement a personal relationship with God.

COME INTO GOD'S PRESENCE
Psalm 63:1; Matthew 6:33; Psalm 100; Psalm 16:11

O God, You are my God. Early will I seek You. I will seek first Your kingdom O God, and Your righteousness; I will make a joyful noise unto You; I will serve You with gladness. I will come before Your presence with singing. I will enter into Your gates with thanksgiving and into Your courts with praise, for You are good; Your mercy is everlasting, and Your truth endures to all generations. I come into Your presence because in Your presence is fullness of joy, and at Your right hand are pleasures forevermore.

CALL ON THE LORDAND CONTINUE STEADFDASTLY IN PRAYER
2 Chronicles 7:14; Psalm 1:2; Jeremiah 29: 12; Genesis 32: 24; Matthew 7:7; 1Chronicles 4:9,10; Luke 18:1; 1 Thessalonians 5:17; Acts 6:4; Colossians 4:2; Acts 1:14; Luke 18:1; Philippians 4:6; James 5:16

I will humble myself and pray and seek Your face, and turn from my wicked ways. I will call upon You and pray to You and You have promised to listen to me. I will meditate on Your law day and night. I will seek You with all my heart and find You, and I will not let go until You bless me. I will ask, seek, and knock, according to Your will and Your word that I might receive what You have for me; that my territory will be enlarged, that I might find all that I need, and that I might see doors open unto me. In obedience to Your word, I will pray always, without ceasing, giving myself continually to prayer and to the ministry of the Word. In everything by prayer and supplication with thanksgiving, I will make my requests known unto You. I will be steadfast and earnest in prayer for the fervent effective prayers of the righteous avail much.

CEASE FROM ALL THAT HINDERS MY CONNECTION WITH THE LORD
Psalm 37 (focus on #8)

I will cease from anger, resentment, evil-thinking, frustration, fretting, grudge-holding, revenge, passive/aggressive behaviors. Rather, I will trust in You, Lord; Delight myself in You, Dwell in Your land and feed on Your faithfulness; Commit my way to You, Rest in You, and Meditate on You day and night.

CAST ASIDE UNNECESSARY HINDRANCES AND PRESS ON
Hebrews 12: 1b; Philippians 3:13, 14

I will lay aside the weights and sins that so easily beset me—gossip, resentment, impatience, intolerance, judgmental attitudes, procrastination—and run with patience the race that is set before me; forgetting those things that are behind, and reaching forward to those things that are ahead, I will press on toward the mark for the prize of the high calling of God in Christ Jesus.

CONFESS MY SIN AND REPENT
Psalm 66:18; 1 John 1:9

If I regard iniquity in my heart, I know that You will not hear me: so I confess my sins (see above) and ask for forgiveness, knowing that if I confess my sins, You are faithful and just to forgive me of my sins and cleanse me of all unrighteousness.

Psalm 51: 1,7,9-12 (David's Prayer of Repentance)

Have mercy upon me, O God, according to your lovingkindness: according to the multitude of your tender mercies blot out my transgressions. Wash me thoroughly from my iniquity, and cleanse me from my sin. Purge me with hyssop, and I shall be clean: wash me, and I shall be whiter than snow. Hide your face from my sins, and blot out all my iniquities. Create in me a clean heart, O God; and renew a right spirit within me. Cast me not away from your presence; and take not your holy spirit from me. Restore unto me the joy of your salvation;

and uphold me with your free spirit. Thank you for forgiveness of sin and transgression.

CHOOSE THE GOOD PART
Luke 10:42

Thank you for the ability to make choices and I choose blessings over burdens; faith over fear. I choose to believe rather than doubt; to trust rather than worry. I choose peace over confusion; joy over sadness. I choose to be powerful rather than powerless; to be hopeful rather than hopeless. I choose courage over cowardice; boldness over timidity; strength over weakness; forgiveness over resentment. I choose to be patient rather than impatient; to love rather than to hate. I choose liberty over captivity; victory over defeat. I choose to be a victor not a victim; a winner not a loser—all choices within my control. The choice is mine and I choose the good part. I have chosen whom I will serve and He has promised that the good part will not be taken from me.

CLING TO THAT WHICH IS GOOD
Romans 12:9; Psalm 100:5; Genesis 50:20; James 1:17

I will cling to You, Lord for You are good. Your mercy is good; Your grace is good; Your love is good; Your compassion is good; Your forgiveness is good. Every good and finite attribute that I can ascribe to You describes and affirms Your goodness. Even those things that the enemy means for evil, You turn them around for good. Every good and perfect gift comes from You, and I will cling to all that is good.

COME CLOSER TO THE LORD
Philippians 3:10; James 4:8

I want a closer walk with You Lord—to walk daily with You in the beauty of holiness. I want to be drawn nearer to You—to the Cross where You died, to Your precious bleeding side, that I may know You and the power of Your resurrection and the fellowship of Your sufferings. I will draw near to You Lord, that You may draw near to me.

CONTINUALLY PRAISE THE LORD
Psalm 34 1-3; Isaiah 61:3

I will bless You, LORD at all times: Your praise will continually be in my mouth. I will magnify You and exalt Your name. When there is a spirit of heaviness, I will put on the garment of praise that You will be exalted and I will be delivered from heaviness to lightness in the spirit. When there is a spirit of laziness, I will put on the garment of praise that You will be glorified and I will be brought out of my lethargy. When there is a spirit of procrastination, I will put on the garment of praise that You will be magnified, and I will be delivered from procrastination to action. When there is a spirit of sleepiness I will put on the garment of praise that You will be lifted up and I will wake up from sleep. When there is a spirit of sadness, I will put on the garment of praise that You will be reverenced and I will be brought from sadness to joy in the spirit. When there is a spirit of pride, I will put on the garment of praise that You will be edified, and I will be delivered from pride and humbled in Your presence. Regardless of circumstances or situations, I will offer to You the sacrifice of praise!

CONSECRATE AND COMMIT MYSELF TO THE LORD
Romans 12: 1,2; Proverbs 3:5,6; John 15:7; Psalm 37:3-8

I will present my body a living sacrifice, holy, acceptable unto You which is my reasonable service. I will trust in You Lord with all my heart. I will not lean unto my own understanding, but in all my ways I will acknowledge You and allow You to direct my paths. I will abide in You, Lord, and let Your words abide in me daily. I will dwell in the land and feed on Your faithfulness. I will delight myself in You, commit my way to You, rest in You, and wait patiently for You.

CONFORM NOT TO, NOR COVET THIS WORLD
Romans 12:2; Ephesians 4:23; 1 John 2:15,16

I will not conform to this world: but I will be transformed by the renewing of my mind, that I may prove what is Your good, and acceptable, and perfect, will for my life. I will be renewed in the spirit of my mind. I will not love the world nor the things in the world—the lust of the flesh, the lust of the eyes, the pride of life—but I will love You with all of my heart, soul, mind and body, and I will obey Your word and do your will.

CAST MY CARES ON THE LORD
1 Peter 5:7; Ephesians 3:20; Isaiah 26:3; Philippians 4:6-8

I will cast all my care on You, Lord for I know that You care for me; and I know that You are able to do exceeding abundantly above all that I ask or think, according to the power that works within me. You will keep me in perfect peace if I keep my mind on You, so today, I will be anxious for nothing but in everything by prayer and supplication with thanksgiving, I will let my requests be made known unto You; and I will let Your peace that surpasses all understanding guard my heart and my mind through Christ Jesus. And I will think (focus) only on those things that are **true, honest, just, pure, lovely, and of good report.**

COVER MYSELF WITH THE BLOOD

Matthew 26:28; Leviticus 17:11; Romans 5:9; Ephesians 1:7;

I plead the blood of Jesus over myself. I figuratively cover myself with Your blood—the blood that You shed for me way back on Calvary. Your precious blood has made atonement for me, washed me, and pardoned my sins. Because there is life in the blood, Your blood is my lifeline to abundant life here, and eternal life hereafter. I am saved by Your blood; I am redeemed by Your blood; I am justified by Your blood; I am healed by Your blood; I am delivered by Your blood; I am protected by Your blood.

COMPLETELY DRESS FOR SUCCESS

Ephesians 6:10-18; 2 Corinthians 10:4-6; Isaiah 54:17; James 4:7

Realizing that I am not wrestling against flesh and blood but against principalities and powers, and against the rulers of the darkness of this world and wickedness in high places, I will put on and use the whole armor of God today—**truth, righteousness, peace, faith, salvation, the Word, and prayer** for this is my protective (offensive) armor as well as my defensive weapons, and the weapons of my warfare are not carnal, but mighty in God to the pulling down of the strongholds of **untruths, unrighteousness, chaos and confusion, fear and frustration, doubt and despair;** casting down imaginations and every high thing that exalts itself against the knowledge of God, bringing every thought into captivity to the obedience of Christ.

This armor (the belt, the breastplate, the shoes, the shield, the helmet and the Sword) is my protection against the tricks, the lies and deceit of the enemy. And because of this armor, no weapon that is formed against me shall prosper, and I can boldly resist the devil and he will flee from me. **IN THE NAME OF JESUS, I AM VICTORIOUS TODAY, HALLELUJAH!**

COMBAT AND CONQUER THE ENEMY
2 Corinthians 4: 8, 9; Romans 8:37-39

There may be times when I am troubled on every side, but I am not distressed; I may be perplexed but I am not in despair; I may be persecuted, but I am not forsaken; I may be cast down, but I am not destroyed, for I am more than a conqueror through You Who loved (and continues to love) me, and I am persuaded, that neither death, nor life, nor angels, nor principalities, nor powers, nor things present, nor things to come, nor height, nor depth, nor any other creature, shall be able to separate me from Your love which is in Christ Jesus our Lord.

CONTINUE IN THE WORK OF THE LORD
Galatians 6:9; 1 Corinthians 15:58;

I will not be weary in well-doing, but I will be steadfast, unmovable, always abounding in Your work and in service to You for I know that in You, my labor is not in vain, and I will reap if I do not faint.

COVENANT WITH GOD TO OBEY HIS COMMANDS
Deuteronomy 28:1-14; 1 Samuel 15:22

I will be obedient to Your word, submit me will to Your will and walk in Your way for obedience is better than sacrifice. I am blessed in the city and blessed in the country; blessed in my going out and blessed in my coming in. I am above and not beneath; I am the head and not the tail; I am a lender and not a borrower. I will not go to the left nor to the right, but I will trust and obey for there's no other way to be happy in Jesus, but to trust and obey.

COMMIT TO CHRISTIAN CONDUCT
Romans 12:1,2, 9-21

I will present my body a living sacrifice, holy and pleasing to You

I will not conform to this world, but be transformed by the renewing of my mind.

I will not think more highly of myself than I ought to think.

I will function in my gifts in proportion to my faith

I will let my love be sincere

I will hate what is evil

I will cling to that which is good I will be devoted to others in brotherly love

I will be devoted to others in brotherly love.

I will honor others above myself

I will not be lacking in zeal, but I will keep spiritual fervor serving the Lord

I will be joyful in hope, patient in affliction, faithful in prayer

I will share with God's people who are in need

I will practice hospitality

I will bless those who persecute me (bless and not curse)

I will rejoice with those who rejoice and mourn (weep) with those who mourn (weep)

I will live in harmony with others

I will not be proud, but willing to associate with people of low position;

I will not be conceited

I will not repay evil for evil

In the eyes of everyone, I will be careful to do what is right

If it is possible, as much as it depends on me, I will live at peace with everyone

I will not seek or take revenge—Vengeance is the Lord's. He will repay

If my enemy is hungry, I'll feed him; if he is thirsty, I'll give him to drink

I will not be overcome by evil, but will overcome evil with good.

COME OUT OF MY COMFORT ZONE
2 Corinthians 5:7; Hebrews 11:6; Matthew 21:21; Luke 5:4; Matthew 14:29; Philippians 4:13; Romans 4:17; Psalm 91:6; 2 Timothy 1:7.

I will walk by faith and not by sight because I know that without faith it is impossible to please You. Lord. I will speak to my "mountains" and then watch You move them out of my way. I will get out of the boat, keep my eyes on You, and walk on the "water" of whatever situation confronts me knowing that by faith, I can do all things through You Who strengthens me. I will launch out into the deep and call those things that be not as though they are. I will not be afraid of the terror by night nor any arrow that flies by day nor any destruction that lays waste at noonday, for You have not given me a spirit of fear, but of power and of love and a of a sound mind.

CONTRIBUTE CHEERFULLY TO THE UPBUILDING OF GOD'S KINGDOM
Malachi 3:10; Luke 6:38; Acts 20:35; Romans 12:6; 2 Corinthians 9:7

I will bring my tithes and offerings into the storehouse that there might be meat in Your house, and You have promised to pour out blessings upon me. I will give cheerfully knowing that it is more blessed to give than to receive, and that You love a cheerful giver. My tithes and offerings are not only of my treasury, but of my time and my talent. I will function in my gifts in proportion to my faith, giving of my best to You that You may use me in Your service.

CONFESS AND CLAIM GOD'S PROMISES FOR MY LIFE
(1 John 5:14, 15).

And this is the confidence I have, that if I ask anything according to Your will, You hear me, and if I know that You hear me, whatever I ask, I know that I have the petitions that I have asked of You. **I am who God says I am; I can have what God says I can have; I can do what God says I can do.**

I have abundant life (John 10:10)

I have access to the You through Jesus Christ, my Lord (John 14:6; Ephesians 3:12)

I have an advocate with You through Jesus Christ, my Lord. (1 John 2:1)

I am blessed (Matthew 5:1-12)

I am blessed with all spiritual blessings in the heavenly places (Ephesians 1:3)

I have blessings that I don't have enough room for, pressed down, shaken together and running over.
(Malachi 3:11; Luke 6:38)

I have holy boldness (Ephesians 3:12; 1 John 4:17)

I am more than a conqueror through Him who loves me (Romans 8:37)

I can do all things through Christ Who strengthens me (Philippians 4:13)

I have eternal (everlasting) life (John 3:16)

I have faith as a grain of mustard seed (Matthew 17:20)

I am forgiven (1 John 1:9)

I am free (John 8:32, 36; Romans 8:2; Galatians 5:1;)

God hears and answers my prayers according to His will (1 John 5:14,15)

Goodness and Mercy follows me every day (Psalm 23:6)

I am healed (mind, soul, body) (Isaiah 53:5)

I am an heir of the Father and joint heirs with the son (Romans 8:17).

I have an intercessor with You through Jesus Christ, my Lord. (Romans 8:26)

I am justified by Your grace (Romans 3:24)

I am a new creation—old things have passed away; all things have become new. (2 Corinthians 5:17)

All of my needs are supplied according to Your riches in glory by Christ Jesus (Philippians 4:19)

I have overcome by the blood of the Lamb (Revelation 12:11)

I have perfect peace—Your peace that surpasses all understanding (Isaiah 26:3; John 14:27; Philippians 4:8)

I am protected from all hurt, harm, and danger (Psalm 46:1; Psalm 91; Isaiah 43:2)

I am redeemed (Galatians 3:13)

I am saved (Romans 10:9,10; Ephesians 2:8,9)

I shall not die but live and declare the works of the Lord (Psalm 118:17)

I am not afraid (2 Timothy 1:7; 1 John 4:18)

I have power (2 Timothy 1:7)

I have renewed strength (Isaiah 40:31)

I have a sound mind (2 Timothy 1:7)

I have a way of escape out of temptation (1 Corinthians 10:12,13)

I have everything I need and I shall not want (Matthew 6:33; Psalm 23:1)

I have fullness of joy, and Your joy is my strength (Psalm 16:11; Nehemiah 8:10c)

APPENDIX B

In this section, make a list of your personal needs and the desires of your heart, then affirm them by faith

CALL THOSE THINGS THAT BE NOT AS THOUGH THEY ARE AND CLAIM THE BLESSINGS OF GOD BY FAITH, NOT BY SIGHT
Romans 4:17; 2 Corinthians 5:7

Suggestions:

Healing for yourself or a loved one. (Enter the names of these persons and pray)

Salvation for a family member or a friend. (Enter the names of these persons and pray)

The return of wandering children, grandchildren, nieces, nephews. (Enter the names of these persons and pray)

A new employment position or a raise in current salary (Pray)

Reversal of some situation that now seems hopeless (Name the situation and pray)

Restoration of a marital relationship (Enter your spouse's name and pray)

APPENDIX C

Daily Checklist of My Personal Christian Behavior

Listed below are 25 questions you might ask yourself at the end of each day as a check and balance of your walk with the Lord. You may add other questions that come to your mind. Make copies of this page, date each page, and check yourself each day. If you cannot answer YES to every question today, don't give up (if at first you don't succeed, try, try again). Tomorrow is another day. Ask God to help you, then yield to His direction and give God a YES!

Date:

Today, did I....

1. Seek first the Kingdom of God and His righteousness?
2. Thank God for all my blessings?
3. Read His word?
4. Pray, Meditate, Wait in the Presence of the Lord?
5. Have on the whole armor?
6. Check each piece and make adjustments wherever necessary?
7. Acknowledge God in all my ways (consult Him about everything)?
8. Allow God to direct my paths (are my steps ordered by the Lord?)
9. Present my body a living sacrifice holy and acceptable unto the Lord?
10. Serenely accept things I couldn't change?
11. Courageously change the things that I could?
12. Choose the difference between the two with wisdom?
13. Love my neighbors as I love myself?
14. Show love to my enemies?
15. Bless those who cursed me?
16. Do good to those who hate me?
17. Pray for those who despitefully use me and persecute me?
18. Do unto others as I would have others do unto me?
19. Forgive others as I have been forgiven?
20. Produce any fruit of the Spirit...Love, Joy, Peace, Long-suffering, Gentleness, Goodness, Faith, Meekness, Self-Control?

21. Allow myself to be transformed by the renewing of my mind?
22. Have the same mind in me that is in Christ Jesus?
23. Walk by faith and not by sight?
24. Do justly, love mercy, and walk humbly with my God?
25. Trust that God would supply all my needs according to His riches in glory?

Notes:

_____

Printed in the United States
65445LVS00002B/193-459

9 781424 159222